Collins

Work on your
Phrasal Verbs

Jamie Flockhart & Cheryl Pelteret

Collins

HarperCollins Publishers
77-85 Fulham Palace Road
Hammersmith
London W6 8JB

First edition 2012

Reprint 10 9 8 7 6 5 4 3 2 1 0

© HarperCollins Publishers 2012

ISBN 978-0-00-746466-1

Collins® is a registered trademark of HarperCollins Publishers Limited

www.collinselt.com

A catalogue record for this book is available from the British Library

Typeset in India by Aptara

Printed in China by South China Printing Co.

About the authors

Jamie Flockhart is a lexicographer and ELT author based in the UK. He taught English in Europe and Asia for several years before going on to work in dictionary and ELT publishing. He has since worked on a broad variety of English language learning materials, including General English and Business English books, and learner dictionaries. Jamie is co-author of *Business Vocabulary in Practice* (Collins, 2012).

Cheryl Pelteret has been involved in language teaching for the past 30 years – as a teacher, editor and writer. She has taught students of all ages and levels in the UK and in Turkey, and has written several course books and a range of supplementary materials for adults, teenagers and young learners. Cheryl is the author of *English for Life: Speaking* (Collins, 2012).

Contents

How to use this book

Welcome to *Work on your Phrasal Verbs!*

Who is this book for?

The book is suitable for:

- intermediate to advanced learners
- learners who are CEF (Common European Framework) level B1+.

You can use the book:

- as a self-study course
- as supplementary material on a general English course.

Book structure

Work on your Phrasal Verbs contains:

- 25 units covering the 400 most common phrasal verbs
- a comprehensive answer key
- appendices which include a study guide with tips to help you remember phrasal verbs and use them correctly
- an index to help you find phrasal verbs quickly and easily.

The phrasal verbs in this book are grouped by topic to make them easier to remember and to help you use and understand them in everyday situations, from chatting with friends to reading a news story. The phrasal verbs are presented alphabetically and in large bold type over two pages in each unit, so that you can see them clearly and find them easily.

Unit structure

Each unit is presented over four pages. The first two pages of each unit present the phrasal verbs, together with full sentence definitions, examples and notes. The second two pages provide exercises to help you practise using the phrasal verbs. Each unit is self-contained, so you can study the units in any order, by selecting the topic you want to study.

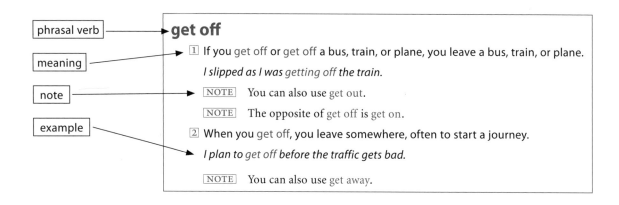

Definitions

The definitions of phrasal verbs are given in full sentences in simple, natural English. This allows you to see the typical patterns and grammatical behaviour of a word, as well as the meaning.

Examples

Each definition is followed by at least one example. All of the examples are taken from the Collins Corpus, a huge database of real language from a variety of sources. The examples have been carefully chosen to show common patterns and typical uses of the phrasal verb, so that you can see how it is really used in English today.

Notes

Notes give you extra information, for example an alternative phrasal verb, or an opposite form.

Informal and formal English

Phrasal verbs are generally more common in spoken or informal English than in written or formal English. However, phrasal verbs can in fact be used in both formal and informal situations.

In this book, both the unit title and the examples given at the phrasal verb can help to show you whether a phrasal verb is more likely to be used in an informal or formal situation.

More **informal** situation:

unit title	phrasal verb	example
Socializing and leisure time	**come along**	*We're going out for dinner. Why don't you come along with us?*

More **formal** situation:

unit title	phrasal verb	example
Reporting in the media	**meet with**	*His comments met with great public approval.*

If a phrasal verb meaning is particularly informal, this is shown after the meaning or in a NOTE.

British and American English

Most of the phrasal verbs in this book are used in both British and American English. However, there are sometimes cases where a phrasal verb or one of its definitions is more usual in either British or American English. This is shown after the meaning or in a NOTE.

Exercises

Each unit contains eight exercises designed to help you practise using all the phrasal verbs from the unit. The examples used in the exercises will help you to understand the phrasal verbs in context and help you to be more confident about using them correctly. You will find answers to all the exercises in the Answer key at the back of the book.

Your turn!

In addition to the exercises, each unit contains a **Your turn!** activity. These are designed to help you find further examples of the phrasal verbs from the unit, or to use the phrasal verbs to talk about your own ideas or experiences.

Other titles

Also available in this range are:

* *Work on your Accent*
* *Work on your Idioms*

Basic actions

1

fall down

If someone or something falls down when they have been in an upright position, they drop to the ground.

He tripped and fell down.

get off

If you get off something that you are on, you move your body from it, usually onto the ground.

He got off his bicycle.

get out

If you get out, you leave a place or a vehicle.

We got out of the car.

get up

1 When someone or something gets up or gets up something, they move from a lower position or level to a higher one.

By the time we'd got up to the top of the hill, we were exhausted.

I knew he would have difficulty getting up those steps.

2 If you get up, you rise to a standing position after you have been sitting or lying down.

He got up off the floor.

3 When you get up, or when someone gets you up, you get out of bed.

She decided it was time to get up.

We had to get the children up and dressed.

go back

If you go back, you return to a place where you were before.

I have to go back to the US next week.

It started to rain so I went back for my umbrella.

go in

When you go in, you enter a building.

Let's go in and have some coffee.

I pushed open the door of the office and went in.

NOTE   The opposite of go in is go out.

go into

When you go into a room, building, or area, you enter it.

She went into the bedroom and shut the door.

go off

If you go off somewhere, you leave the place where you were, usually in order to do something.

He's gone off to work.

keep down

If you keep down or if you keep your head down, you stay in a lying or low position in order to avoid being seen or attacked.

The soldier signalled to him to keep down.

lay down

If you lay something down, you put it down on a surface.

He laid the baby gently down on the changing table.

move up

If someone or something moves up or moves up a place, they go from a lower position to a higher one.

The sun had moved up in the sky

We moved up the hill a few metres.

NOTE   The opposite of move up is move down.

run in

If someone runs in from outside a room or building, they enter it, moving fast.

I'll run in and get them.

run into

To run into a place means to enter it running.

They had run into the nearest apartment and asked for help.

run on

If you run on, you continue to run in the same direction.

I ran on ahead.

run out

1 If you run out of a room or building, you leave it, running.

He ran out of the room and down the stairs.

2 If a substance runs out from somewhere, it flows from there.

Water was running out from under the front door of the house.

sit down

If you sit down or sit yourself down, you lower your body until you are sitting on something.

We were both looking for a place to sit down.

She sat herself down beside me.

NOTE   The opposite of sit down is stand up.

stand up

If you stand up, you change your position so that you are standing rather than sitting or lying.

The pupils stand up when the teacher comes into the room.

NOTE   You can also use get up.

turn back

If you turn back or are turned back, you stop a journey and return towards the place you started from.

It was getting dark, so we turned back.

We were turned back by heavy snow.

Exercise 1

Match verbs 1–5 with particles A–E to make phrasal verbs from this unit.

1 stand / move / get
2 lay / sit / keep
3 run / get
4 go / turn
5 run / go

A back
B out
C down
D into
E up

Exercise 2

Complete the sentences. Choose the correct particles.

1 We enjoyed it and would really like to go *on / in / back* one day.
2 Could you run *into / away / in* and get my glasses?
3 It started raining so they turned *out / on / back* and went home.
4 Chloe went *on / off / into* the shop and bought some water.
5 Grandma walked slowly, but the children ran *on / with / onto*.
6 Zack went *onto / with / in* and ordered a drink.

Exercise 3

Match sentence halves 1–6 with A–F to make complete sentences.

1 Mrs Todd came running out
2 A lot of the people
3 I remember running into
4 I went back to the kitchen
5 The pile of books fell down
6 We had until 7:15

A to get ourselves up.
B and scattered all over the floor.
C were turned back at the border.
D and stood at the side of the road.
E the playroom in tears.
F to continue cooking.

Exercise 4

Match each phrasal verb 1–4 with its opposite meaning A–D.

1 go in
2 move up
3 sit down
4 run in

A move down
B stand up
C run out
D go out

Exercise 5

Choose the best answer to complete the sentences.

1 After a while we all *sat down / stood up / fell down* to eat.
2 Someone *fell down / stood up / went into* in the middle of the hall and asked a question.
3 She *went into / sat down / got up* and walked across the room.
4 She *laid the book down / moved the book up / ran the book out* on the table.
5 I *ran out / sat down / went into* and slammed the door.
6 I need to *get off / get out / turn back* of New York for a while.

Exercise 6

Complete the sentences with the correct form of the phrasal verbs in the box.

| get off | run in | move up | lay down | get up | get out |

1 Brody _____ of bed at 8:30 this morning.
2 I need to _____ early tomorrow for work.
3 He _____ through the open door and sat down in the living room.
4 I saw something _____ that tree over there.
5 I took a fifty dollar bill and _____ it _____ on the counter.
6 He _____ his stool and went to the door.

Work on your Phrasal Verbs Basic actions

Exercise 7

Make these sentences less formal. Replace the <u>underlined</u> words with the phrasal verbs in the box.

| get up | go back | go into | move down | sit down | turn back |

1 I forgot my glasses, so I had to <u>stop and return home</u> to fetch them.
2 Please do not <u>enter</u> the building without a permit.
3 In the winter, the goats <u>descend</u> the mountains from the high ground.
4 Are you planning to <u>return</u> to the UK after your trip abroad?
5 If you find it difficult to <u>ascend</u> the stairs, you are welcome to use the lift.
6 Please <u>take a seat</u>.

Exercise 8

Read the following safety advice from a ski resort website. <u>Underline</u> all the phrasal verbs, then decide if the sentences that follow are true (*T*) or false (*F*).

SKI SAFELY

* You must always sit down while using the chairlift.
* If you fall down on the slope, or if you fall from the chairlift, do not get up too quickly.
* If you fall from the chair lift, keep your head down until it is safe to stand up again.
* If you think you may be injured, lay your skis down on the ground and wait for help.
* Always stay with another person. Do not go off on your own.
* If it starts to snow heavily, you should consider turning back.

1 Always stand up on the chairlift. ☐ F
2 If you are injured, ski to someone and ask for help. ☐ T
3 It is safe to ski alone. ☐ F
4 If it snows heavily, leave the slopes and return to
   your accommodation. ☐ T
5 If you fall from the chairlift, get up quickly. ☐ F
6 Keep you head down while on the chairlift. ☐ F

Your turn!

Look for a website that gives advice about a sport or activity you'd like to try and find examples of the phrasal verbs in this unit.

It was hard for his mother
to get him up in the morning.

Actions with an object

let in

If you let someone in, you allow them to come into a place, usually by opening the door for them.

We rang the doorbell and someone came and let us in.

light up

To light something up means to shine light on or in it, so that it is bright and easy to see.

The match lit up her face.

look for

If you look for something or someone, you try to find them.

Someone came to the office looking for you.

pick up

If you pick something or someone up, you lift them up from a surface.

The baby was crying so I picked her up.

NOTE   You can also use lift up.

put back

If you put something back somewhere, you put it in the place it was in before it was moved.

Shall I put it back in the box for you?

put down

If you put down someone or something that you are holding or carrying, you put them on the floor or on a table, bed, etc.

He put the basket down and looked inside it.

She put down her case and kissed him.

NOTE   You can also use set down.

NOTE   The opposite of put down is pick up.

put in

If you put something in or put one thing in another, you put one thing inside another thing.

I need to put a new battery in.

He stood at the slot machine and put in a coin.

put together

If you put together an object or its parts, you join its parts to each other so that it can be used.

It's very interesting to see how they put together these huge structures.

I have all the parts here – I just need to put them together.

NOTE   The opposite of put together is take apart.

put up

If you put something up, you move it to a higher position.

He put up the collar of his jacket.

Anna put her feet up on the desk.

take away

If you take something away from a place or position, you remove it from a place and put it somewhere else.

She took her hands away from her eyes and looked.

A waiter came to take away the plates.

NOTE   The opposite of take away is put back.

take back

When you take something back, you take it to the place where you were before or where it was before.

I filled a plastic bottle with water and took it back to the car.

take into

If you take someone or something into a place, you go with them there.

I'll take you into town if you like.

throw at

If you throw an object at someone or something, you try to hit them with the object by throwing it.

He threw a dart at the board.

throw away

If you throw something away, you get rid of it because you no longer want or need it.

I can make soup with the leftover chicken, so don't throw it away.

throw in

If you throw something in or throw it in something, you casually put or drop it into something such as a container or mixture.

Add a teaspoonful of salt, and throw in the rice.

'Have you got room for my bag in your car?' – 'Sure, throw it in.'

I threw it in a drawer and forgot about it.

throw out

1 If you throw out something, you throw it so that it moves quickly away from you.

The fishermen threw the net out and could not pull it back in.

She threw out handfuls of corn for the chickens.

2 If you throw out something you no longer want, you get rid of it.

They threw out their rubbish.

NOTE   You can also use throw away.

turn off

If you turn off a device or machine, you make it stop working using its controls. If it turns off, it stops working.

George came in and turned off the radio.

The heating turns off automatically at night.

NOTE   You can also use switch off.

NOTE   The opposite of turn off is turn on.

turn on

If you turn a device or machine on, you make it start working using its controls. If it turns on, it starts working.

Shall I turn the lights on?

The tap won't turn on.

NOTE   You can also use switch on.

Exercise 1

Match verbs 1–6 with particles A–F to make phrasal verbs from this unit.

1	let / throw / put	A	away
2	light / pick	B	back
3	put / take	C	for
4	throw / take	D	in
5	put	E	together
6	look	F	up

Exercise 2

Complete the sentences. Choose the correct particles.

1 Maya picked the bags *on / in / up* and left the restaurant.
2 He took the suitcases *down / back / into* upstairs.
3 I took my cup of coffee *into / over / under* the living room.
4 The children threw snowballs *on / in / at* each other.
5 He turned *on / in / away* the shower.
6 Tommy helped me put my new desk *on / out / together*.
7 Jennifer put her glass *with / away / down* on the table.
8 Put your hand *up / over / with* if you know the answer.

Exercise 3

Decide if the following sentences are true (*T*) or false (*F*).

1 If you let someone in, you allow them to leave a place. ☐
2 If you light something up, you shine light on or in it. ☐
3 If you put something back, you move it to a new place. ☐
4 If you throw something in, you drop it into something. ☐
5 If you turn something off, you make it start working. ☐
6 If you take something away, you take it to the place where it was before. ☐
7 If you put something down, you put it on the floor or on a table etc. ☐
8 If you put something up, you move it to a lower position. ☐

Exercise 4

Match each phrasal verb 1–5 with another phrasal verb A–E that has the same meaning.

1	turn off	A	throw away
2	pick up	B	switch on
3	throw out	C	switch off
4	turn on	D	lift up
5	put down	E	set down

Exercise 5

Match sentence halves 1–6 with A–F to make complete sentences.

1	I don't need this jacket anymore	A	as long as you put it back on my bookshelf afterwards.
2	I'm going to take this iron back to the shop	B	because it doesn't work properly.
3	To save electricity, turn off the lights	C	can you let me in?
4	I've forgotton my key –	D	please pick it up.
5	You can borrow my dictionary	E	so I'm going to throw it out.
6	You dropped some litter –	F	when you leave a room.

Exercise 6

Match questions 1–6 with answers A–F.

1 Are you looking for something in particular?
2 Where did you find that interesting coin?
3 Have you seen my wallet?
4 Did you put my pen back in my pencil case?
5 May I take away your plates?
6 Shall we watch the news on TV?

A Yes, I'll turn it on.
B Yes, I did. Thanks for lending it to me.
C I just picked it up in the street. It's dated 1954!
D Yes, thank you. It was a delicious meal.
E Yes – a present for my mother.
F I think you put it in your coat pocket.

Exercise 7

Make these sentences less formal. Replace the <u>underlined</u> verbs with the phrasal verbs in the box.

| lit up | put together | looking for | throw away | let in | put back |

1 The management will only <u>admit</u> people who have tickets.
2 She <u>replaced</u> the phone.
3 The sun <u>illuminated</u> the sky.
4 It takes eight hours to <u>assemble</u> each device.
5 She decided to <u>discard</u> her old shoes.
6 We are <u>seeking</u> a new car.

Exercise 8

Read Jessica's Internet messages about her trip to Tokyo. <u>Underline</u> all the phrasal verbs, then answer the questions.

- I arrived very late at the hotel last night, and the doors were locked. Thankfully one of the hotel workers let me in!
- I wasn't sure at first how to turn on the shower in the hotel. Then I spent half an hour looking for the switch to turn it off!
- Tokyo looks amazing! At night the city is completely lit up with neon lights.
- It's great that I can just put a coin in the machine and then choose a hot or ice cold coffee!

1 Who let Jessica in to the hotel?
2 Why could she not let herself in?
3 What did she have difficulty turning on?
4 How long did it take her to turn the shower off?
5 What lights up the city at night?
6 What does Jessica need to put in the machine to get a coffee?

Your turn!

Think about what you did one day last week. Use the phrasal verbs in this unit to describe your or another person's actions with an object. For example:

I picked up my briefcase from my desk.

A waitress took away my empty cup.

13

3

Movement and change

bring up

If you bring up a child, you look after it until it is grown up and you try to give it particular beliefs.

His parents brought him up to believe it was possible to achieve anything.

come along

1. When someone comes along or comes along a road or other area of ground, they move along somewhere towards you.

   They're coming along behind us, I think.

2. When something or someone comes along, they start to happen or exist.

   This was the greatest advance until X-rays came along in the 1890s.

3. If something or someone is coming along, they are making progress or developing in the way you want.

   The arrangements are coming along nicely.

   NOTE   You can also use come on.

come back

When someone or something comes back, they return to the place where they were before.

I've just come back from the hairdresser's.

come down

When someone or something comes down or comes down something, they move from a higher position to a lower one.

We met them as they were coming down the hill.

come in

When someone comes in, they enter the room or building where you are.

She came in and sat on the edge of the bed.

come off

If someone or something comes off or comes off an area, place, or vehicle, they leave it.

Their goalkeeper had to come off with an injury.

She saw him come off the plane.

come out

When someone comes out of their house or room, or a place where they were hidden, they leave it or appear from it.

I saw them go into the building and come out five minutes later.

come through

When someone comes through, they move out of one room and enter another.

The doctor can see you now if you would like to come through.

come up

When someone or something comes up or comes up something, they move from a lower position to a higher one, or move towards the place where you are.

I could hear him coming up the stairs.

get back

1 If you get back, you return somewhere after being in another place.

What time do you usually get back from work?

2 If you get something back, you get it again after losing it or giving it to someone else.

I'm going to return it to the shop and get my money back.

go over

When you go over, you move towards someone or something and reach them.

I went over to congratulate the parents.

grow up

1 When a child grows up, they gradually change into being an adult.

I grew up in New York.

2 If you tell an adult to grow up, you are telling them in an angry way to stop behaving in a silly or childish way. [INFORMAL]

You're upset because she's giving the baby more attention than you? Grow up, Gene!

leave behind

If you leave someone or something behind, you do not take them with you when you go somewhere.

The box wouldn't fit in the car, so we had to leave it behind.

make for

If you make for a place, you move towards it in a quick or determined way.

The best thing would be to make for high ground.

NOTE   You can also use head for.

move in

When you move in, you begin to live in a house or place.

I've got the keys and I'm moving in on Saturday.

NOTE   The opposite of move in is move out.

return to

When you return to a place, you go back there after you have been away.

I returned to my hotel.

run down

To run down somewhere means to run to a lower level or away from a place.

She ran down the steps.

start out

1 If you start out, you begin to move and go somewhere.

They started out early the next morning.

NOTE   You can also use set off, set out, and start off.

2 To start out means to begin something in a particular way or by doing a particular thing.

He started out in his early twenties with a small shop.

NOTE   You can also use start off.

NOTE   The opposite of start out is end up.

Exercise 1

Complete the sentences. Choose the correct particles.

1 Anjelica was brought *off / up / for* by strict parents.
2 After driving for a while, we came *out / in / through* of the tunnel.
3 Leo left the room and came *along / behind / back* with his laptop.
4 This kind of opportunity doesn't often come *down / along / over*.
5 When did you get *over / on / back* from your holiday?
6 Ashley grew *up / out / away* in a small town outside Brisbane.

Exercise 2

Match sentence halves 1–6 with A–F to make complete sentences.

1 I'm determined to get	A and said hello.
2 He went over to her	B down the stairs.
3 When we moved in, the house	C my money back.
4 When the game finished, we started	D out for home.
5 She found an umbrella in the station	E that someone had left behind.
6 He ran	F had no furniture.

Exercise 3

Decide if the following sentences are true (*T*) or false (*F*).

1 If you come in, you enter a place. ☐
2 If you come off, you leave a place. ☐
3 If you come out of a place, you enter it. ☐
4 If you come through, you leave one room and enter another. ☐
5 If you come up, you move from a high position to a lower one. ☐
6 If you come down, you move from a low position to a higher one. ☐

Exercise 4

Complete the sentences with the phrasal verbs in the box.

coming off	came in	returned to	come through	coming up	made for

1 Why don't you _____ to the living room to watch TV?
2 When he _____ he looked tired.
3 We watched the passengers _____ the boat.
4 She could see a large tractor _____ the hill.
5 After the film finished, we _____ the exit.
6 Adam _____ the library a week later.

Exercise 5

Complete the sentences with the correct form of the phrasal verbs in the box.

come along	start out	get ... back	go over	come back

1 Maria has just _____ from a holiday in China.
2 His phone made a beeping noise, so he _____ and picked it up.
3 How is your research programme _____?
4 I _____ as a technician, but now I'm a manager.
5 She lent him a pen, but she didn't _____ it _____.

Exercise 6

Correct the phrasal verbs in these sentences.

1 Where were you grown up?
2 It took the passengers a long time to come out the plane.
3 The explorer started up on a journey to Asia.
4 After many years, he ended out having travelled around the world.
5 If it starts raining, go for the forest – we can shelter there.
6 The holidays are over and it's time to return back college.

Exercise 7

Match the <u>underlined</u> phrasal verbs 1–6 with a word or phrase A–F with the same meaning.

1 If you get lost, just <u>go up to</u> a local person and ask for directions
2 What time do you usually <u>get back</u> from work?
3 He was seriously injured in a bicycle accident, but he's <u>coming along</u> nicely.
4 If you aren't happy with the product, you can <u>get</u> your money <u>back</u>.
5 We're going to live in a different town. We're <u>moving out</u> at the end of the month.
6 Can you believe it – the day before my holiday, and I'm <u>coming down with</u> a terrible cold.

A get something back again after giving it to someone
B making good progress
C starting to get
D return
E approach
F leaving this place

Exercise 8

Read this extract from Reza's blog, where he talks about how his life has changed. <u>Underline</u> all the phrasal verbs, then answer the questions.

I grew up in a small village. When I was still young, my father didn't come back from the war, so my mother had to bring me up on her own. When I was older, I had to leave my mother behind to look for work in the city. But I knew I could return to the village to visit my family and friends. When I started out living in the city, I had no money. But now I have my own small software company, and the business is really coming along. In fact I've just bought a new house and I can't wait to move in!

1 Where did Reza grow up?
2 Who didn't come back from the war?
3 Who brought Reza up?
4 Why did Reza have to leave his mother behind?
5 Is Reza's business successful?
6 Is Reza living in the house he has just bought?

Your turn!

What things have changed in your life? Use the phrasal verbs in this unit to talk about them. For example:

I grew up in a city but now I live on a farm.

My football skills have come along since I started playing.

They **grow up** so fast these days.

Communication

4

ask for

1 If you ask for something, you say that you would like to have it.

She asked for a drink of water.

2 If you ask for someone when you are making a phone call, you say that you would like to speak to them.

He rang the office and asked for Cynthia.

call back

1 If you call back, you go to see someone briefly for a second time.

I'll call back tomorrow and collect the shoes.

2 If you call back, you telephone someone for a second time.

I'll call back when you're not so busy.

3 If you call someone back, you telephone them again in return for a telephone call they have made to you.

Can I call you back later?

NOTE   You can also use ring back. This is mainly British.

call up

If you call up or call someone up, you telephone someone.

Paul often calls me up just for a chat.

She called up an old boyfriend to invite him out for dinner.

The radio station had an open line on which listeners could call up to discuss various issues.

NOTE   You can also use phone up and ring up.

come back to

If you come back to a particular subject, you mention or start to discuss it again.

We always come back to the same point.

get back to

1 If you get back to what you were doing or talking about before, you start doing it or talking about it again.

I couldn't get back to sleep.

NOTE   You can also use go back to.

2 If you get back to someone, you contact them again after a short period of time.

Leave a message and I'll get back to you.

hang on

If you hang on, you wait for a short time. [INFORMAL]

Hang on a minute, I'm not ready.

NOTE   You can also use hold on.

hear from

If you hear from someone or hear something from them, you receive a phone call, email, or other message from them.

I don't hear from my sister very often.

Have you heard anything from Oliver since he went to university?

hold back

If you hold back, or if something holds you back, you do not do or say something that you want to do or say.

She always says exactly what she thinks, without holding back.

She wanted to ask his name, but something held her back.

hold on

[1] If you hold on, you wait or stop what you are doing for a short time.

Hold on! I can't hear you if you all talk at once!

NOTE   You can also use hang on.

[2] If you ask someone you are speaking to on the phone to hold on, you want them to wait for a short time.

Hold on a moment, please, I'll put you through.

make out

[1] If you make something out, you manage to see or hear it.

He could just make out the number plate of the car.

She was mumbling something but I couldn't make it out.

NOTE   You can also use pick out.

[2] If you make something out, you manage to understand it.

I can't make out if Lily likes him or not.

The essay was full of complex ideas and we struggled to make them out.

NOTE   You can also use work out.

[3] If you make out that something is true, you try to make people believe it.

He tried to make out he'd forgotten, but I knew he hadn't.

put to

If you put something to someone, you say it to them in order to find out how they react to it.

These are the sort of questions that I'll be putting to the politicians.

talk to

If you talk to someone, you have a conversation with them.

I just wanted to talk to you.

NOTE   You can also use talk with.

talk with

If you talk with someone, you have a conversation with them. [mainly AMERICAN]

I'd like to talk with you about your husband.

turn down

If you turn something or someone down, you refuse a request or offer.

She applied for a job in a restaurant, but was turned down.

He asked me to help and I couldn't really turn him down.

Exercise 1

Complete the sentences with the words in the box.

back | back to | for

1 We'll come _____ that point later on.
2 She called the number and asked _____ the manager.
3 Hiroto was keen to get _____ work.
4 Something held her _____ from saying anything.
5 He always asked _____ a receipt.
6 I'll call you _____ with more details later.

Exercise 2

Complete the sentences. Choose the correct particles.

1 Would you mind holding *out / on / back* while I call Mr Smith?
2 He's not here at the moment. Can I ask him to call you *up / back / out*?
3 I'll get *back / out / on* to you soon with my decision.
4 The photo is very unclear – I can't make it *out / up / over* very well.
5 He asked her to go to the cinema with him but she turned him *out / back / down*.
6 I've got a proposal I'd like to put *through / to / with* you.

Exercise 3

Match phrasal verbs 1–6 with definitions A–F.

1 turn down   A manage to see or hear something
2 make out   B wait for a short time
3 come back to   C refuse a request or offer
4 hang on   D receive a message from someone
5 hold back   E not say or do something you want to
6 hear from   F mention something again

Exercise 4

Match sentence halves 1–6 with A–F to make complete sentences.

1 I called her up last night   A to ask how she was.
2 We haven't heard   B turn down the offer.
3 I really need to talk to   C what the sign said.
4 It was dark and it was hard to make out   D from him in a long time.
5 I put it to him that he might make E you about something.
6 In the end he decided to   F money from the scheme.

Exercise 5

Replace the <u>underlined</u> phrasal verbs with one from the box with the same meaning.

called ... back | call up | get back to | hang on | make out | talk to

1 Can we <u>go back to</u> the point you raised earlier?
2 I can't <u>work out</u> why he did it.
3 I <u>rang</u> Stefan <u>back</u> the following day.
4 Can you <u>hold on</u> for a minute or two?
5 Can I <u>talk with</u> you about this?
6 You can <u>phone up</u> and speak to an adviser at any time.

Exercise 6

Read the following text message conversation. <u>Underline</u> **all the phrasal verbs, then match them with the correct definitions 1–6.**

> **Katy:** Hi Ying! Sorry I had to go earlier on the phone. My mum was trying to talk to me from downstairs and I couldn't make out what she was saying.
>
> **Ying:** That's OK! Thanks for getting back to me. I just called you up to ask you for some advice.
>
> **Katy:** I'm busy right now, but can you call me back at 7 p.m.?
>
> **Ying:** Sure. We'll speak then!

1 telephone someone
2 say you would like to have something
3 manage to hear something
4 telephone someone for a second time
5 contact someone again after a short time
6 have a conversation with someone

Exercise 7

Complete the sentences with the correct form of the phrasal verbs in the box.

| make out | hang on | come back to | turn down | put ... to | hold back |

1 Sorry, I couldn´t _____ what you said there. Can you repeat that?
2 I'm afraid I'm going to have to _____ your offer.
3 Let's _____ that question a bit later.
4 Would you mind _____ a moment?
5 I usually don't _____: I say what I mean.
6 He _____ it _____ her that she had done this deliberately.

Exercise 8

Read the extract from an email to an online shopping company. <u>Underline</u> **all the phrasal verbs, then answer the questions.**

> I'd like to make a complaint about your customer service. I was told that if there was a problem with my order, I should call up the customer service department and talk to someone about it. Well, when someone eventually answered the phone, I was told to hold on while they found my details. After half an hour of hanging on, nobody had got back to me, so I ended the call. I was hoping to hear from you again but nobody has called me back yet. I might have to put my complaint to them in writing now.

1 Who did the caller want to have a conversation with?
2 What did the caller have to do for a long time, after someone answered the call?
3 How long did the caller have before ending the phone call?
4 What did the caller expect would happen after ending the phone call?
5 Has the caller had any response from the company?
6 What does the caller intend to do next?

Your turn!

Do you prefer to send messages or speak to people on the phone? Use the phrasal verbs in this unit to talk about the different ways you communicate.
For example:

I like talking to my friends on the phone.

Hang on while I update my blog!

5

Giving information

base on

If you base one thing on another thing, or if it is based on another thing, it takes its general form, subject or ideas from that other thing.

I based my novel on my experiences as a nurse.

Many educational systems are based on this model.

NOTE You can also use base upon. This form is more formal.

begin with

1 If you begin with something, you deal with it or do it first.

We should perhaps begin with the issue of staffing.

2 If something that is printed or written begins with a particular letter, word, or sentence, this letter, word, or sentence is its first part.

Think of all the names beginning with D.

bring up

If you bring up a particular subject, you start talking about it.

I advised her to bring the matter up at the next meeting.

I am sorry to bring up the subject of politics yet again.

come up with

If you come up with a plan, idea, or solution, you think of it and suggest it.

It didn't take her long to come up with a very convincing example.

cut out

If you cut out part of something that someone has written, you remove it from the text and do not print or broadcast it.

He cut out all references to the prince being ugly.

Her publishers had cut several stories out of her memoirs.

deal with

If something such as a book, film or discussion deals with a particular topic or idea, it discusses, explains or expresses it.

These questions will be dealt with in Chapter 7.

fill in

1 If you fill in a document or the information on a document, you write all the information that is needed on it. [BRITISH]

We will fill the invoices in with all the necessary information.

Fill in your name and address here.

NOTE You can also use fill out.

2 If you fill someone in, you give them information about something.

I'll fill you in on the details now.

leave out

If you leave someone or something out, you do not include them in something.

One or two scenes in the play were left out of the film.

I invited the whole class because I didn't want to leave anyone out.

move on to

If you move on to a topic, you start talking about it after talking about something else.

By the time I returned, the conversation had moved on to other matters.

NOTE   You can also use move onto, turn to and come on to.

put forward

If you put forward an idea or plan, you state it or publish it so that people can consider it and discuss it.

The theory was first put forward by scientists in the US.

She planned to put her suggestions forward at the next meeting.

NOTE   You can also use set out.

refer to

If you refer to a particular subject or person, you talk about them or mention them.

In his letters to Vita he rarely referred to political events.

start off

To start something off means to cause it to begin.

It was Terry who started off the argument.

I asked a simple question to start the interview off.

sum up

1 If you sum something up, you briefly describe its most important aspects.

I can't sum up his whole philosophy in one sentence.

To sum all this up: what we need is a reform of the system.

2 If someone sums up, they briefly repeat the main points of a speech or debate as a conclusion.

At the end of the discussion, he summed up, and added a few points.

write in

1 If you write in, you send a letter to an organization.

We are offering a half-price holiday to the first person to write in with the correct explanation.

2 If you write in a piece of information on a form or document, you add the information by writing it in the correct place.

Don't forget to write in your name and address on the form.

He arranged the meeting for Tuesday and wrote it in on the calendar in red pen.

Exercise 1

Complete the sentences. Choose the correct particles.

1 The book begins *out / with / on* an introduction to the topic.
2 I want to start the discussion *off / in / forward* with my own view on this.
3 She helps me to come *out with / over with / up with* new ideas.
4 Andrew deliberately left *out / on / with* some of the details.
5 He was referring *in / on / to* his previous job.
6 Keira summed the film *up / on / in* as dull and uninteresting.
7 Could you fill *with / on / out* this form, please?
8 She wrote *in / on / out* to the TV show to ask for more details.

Exercise 2

Match phrasal verbs 1–6 with definitions A–F.

1 If something is based on something, it
2 If a film deals with a topic, it
3 If you put forward an idea, you
4 If you leave something out, you
5 If you come up with something, you
6 If you fill someone in, you

A takes its ideas from that thing.
B do not include it.
C think of it and suggest it.
D explains or expresses it.
E state it or publish it.
F give them information about something.

Exercise 3

Match sentence halves 1–8 with A–H to make complete sentences.

1 I wrote a report based
2 The film deals
3 To sum up: within our society
4 Let's now move on to
5 I hope to come
6 Her name begins
7 I filled him
8 Sorry, I didn't mean to bring up such

A the topic of voting behaviour.
B with the letter A.
C on the information you gave me.
D there still exist major inequalities.
E with the conflicts between two generations of a family.
F up with some of the answers.
G a painful subject.
H in on what happened earlier.

Exercise 4

Choose the best answers to complete the sentences.

1 The prize will go to the first person who *leaves out / puts forward / writes in* with the correct answer.
2 It's a difficult issue to *bring up / base on / write in*.
3 I'll *cut out / begin with / write in* a report about our most important products.
4 They always *referred to / moved onto / summed up* him by his surname.
5 He *brings the job up / sums the job up / comes up with the job* as 'managing change'.
6 I *based on / started off / cut out* the project by finding information on the Internet.

Exercise 5

Correct the phrasal verbs in these sentences.

1 The findings are based in five years of scientific research.
2 Ahmed had come off with another good idea.
3 All confidential details have been cut forward of the report.
4 Dana didn't want to leave off any important details.
5 I would sum on the show as dull and predictable.
6 She refers off him as her partner.

Exercise 6

Complete the sentences with the phrasal verbs in the box.

| based on | began with | come up with | put forward | started off | wrote ... in |

1 Jack _____ the answer _____ carefully.
2 Anna _____ a brief overview of the situation.
3 The new film is _____ a true story.
4 The company are trying to _____ a new game.
5 Theo had _____ a very strong argument.
6 What _____ the fight?

Exercise 7

Make these sentences sound less formal. Replace the <u>underlined</u> verbs with the phrasal verbs in the box.

| based on | leave out | put forward | cut out | dealt with | sums up |

1 The report <u>encapsulates</u> the arguments for and against this plan.
2 This question is <u>discussed</u> in the next chapter.
3 The following film is <u>based upon</u> true events.
4 He <u>stated</u> several suggestions at the meeting.
5 She <u>removed</u> the last few paragraphs.
6 You can <u>omit</u> this part.

Exercise 8

Read the following advice about writing a report. <u>Underline</u> all the phrasal verbs, then decide if the sentences that follow are true (*T*) or false (*F*).

> Your report should be based on factual evidence. Begin with a short introduction in which you put forward your main argument. You can leave out smaller details at this point. Then move onto your first topic. Try to come up with at least three topics which deal with different areas. If there are more than five areas, you may wish to cut out some of them or refer to them only briefly. To finish your report, sum up the main points and give a short conclusion.

1 The introduction is when you put forward your first topic. ☐
2 You should begin with a short conclusion. ☐
3 You can leave out small details. ☐
4 The report should be based on facts. ☐
5 You should come up with at least three topics. ☐
6 To finish, you should sum up the main points. ☐
7 You can cut out the conclusion. ☐
8 The report should deal with at least six areas. ☐

Your Turn!

Look for a website that gives advice about writing reports. Can you find any examples of the phrasal verbs in this unit?

She decided not to **bring up** the subject of global politics again.

6

Planning and organizing

aim at

[1] If you aim at something, or if something that you do is aimed at having a particular effect, you hope to achieve it.

They are aiming at a higher production level.

The research is aimed at developing treatments for the disease.

[2] If an action or activity is aimed at someone, it is intended to influence them or be of interest or help to them.

Many of the devices are aimed at people with hearing problems.

NOTE You can also use be directed at.

count on

If you count on something, you expect it to happen and include it in your plans.

These workers can now count on a regular salary.

NOTE You can also use count upon and rely on.

end up

If you end up in a particular place or situation, you are in that place or situation after a series of events, even though you did not originally intend to be.

If we go on in this way, we'll end up with millions of people unemployed.

NOTE You can also use wind up and finish up.

fit in

If you manage to fit in a person or task, you manage to find time to deal with them.

I'm on holiday next week, but I can fit you in on the 9th.

NOTE You can also use squeeze in.

follow up

[1] If you follow something up, you try to find out more about it and perhaps do something about it.

When I heard the rumours, I tried to follow them up.

[2] If you follow up one action or thing with another, you do or have the second action or thing soon after the first.

They must attend the course, and this is followed up by personal visits.

The President followed up the first round of voting by challenging his opponent to a public debate.

go about

If you go about a task or problem in a particular way, that is the way you start to deal with it.

I'd been wondering how to go about it.

line up

If you line something or someone up in preparation for an event or activity, you arrange for them to be ready and available.

We've lined someone up to present the show.

I had plenty of questions lined up for him.

plan for

If you plan for a particular thing or event, you consider it when you are making your arrangements.

Why didn't I plan for this possibility?

pull off

If you pull something off, you succeed in doing something difficult.

They pulled off a deal with an Australian firm.

She had succeeded, triumphantly: she had pulled it off.

rule out

If you rule out something or someone, you decide that they are impossible or unsuitable or that they are not responsible for something.

The government has not ruled out military action.

You have to be under thirty, so that rules me out.

run into

If you run into problems or difficulties, you unexpectedly begin to experience them.

He ran into trouble with his economic policies.

set out

1 If you set out to do something, you intend and begin to do it.

They had failed in what they had set out to do.

2 If you set something out, you explain facts or ideas clearly in writing or in speech.

His conclusions were set out in his article.

start on

If you start on something, you begin doing it or doing something with it.

You clean the kitchen while I start on the bathroom.

turn out

If something turns out a particular way, it happens in that way.

It turned out to be a really great evening.

NOTE You can also use work out.

wind up

1 When you wind up an activity or event, or when an activity or event winds up, it ends.

When my turn came to wind up the debate, I felt very nervous.

Perhaps we should wind it up there.

2 If you wind up in a particular place or situation, you are in it as the end result of a series of events or processes.

After a great night out we wound up at a Chinese restaurant.

This plan might wind up costing us more money.

NOTE You can also use finish up and end up.

Exercise 1

Match the particles in the box with the verbs to make phrasal verbs from this unit.

out | up | into | on

1 end / follow / line / wind _____
2 rule / set / turn _____
3 count / start _____
4 run _____

Exercise 2

Complete the sentences with the particles in the box.

up | out | on | for | about | off

1 They can't rule _____ the possibility of a takeover.
2 I think you may have gone _____ this the wrong way.
3 When the business collapsed, we ended _____ with no money.
4 The team pulled _____ a win against Spain.
5 We always plan _____ several different outcomes.
6 I'm glad I can count _____ your support.

Exercise 3

Match each phrasal verb 1–5 with another phrasal verb A–E that has the same meaning.

1 turn out   A be directed at
2 fit in   B work out
3 end up   C rely on
4 count on   D squeeze in
5 be aimed at   E wind up

Exercise 4

Match phrasal verbs 1–6 with a word or phrase A–F with the same meaning.

1 The advertising campaign is aimed at women.   A arranged
2 We could probably fit you in some time next week.   B ended up
3 The band has another tour lined up for this summer.   C find time to deal with you
4 We always follow up any customer complaints.   D intended to influence
5 He wound up in hospital after the accident.   E begin doing
6 I'll start on the accounts now.   F investigate

Exercise 5

Complete the sentences. Choose the correct answer.

1 If you wind something up, you *start / finish* it.
2 If you follow something up, you *take something from it / find out more or do more about it*.
3 If you pull something off, you *are / aren't* successful.
4 If something is ruled out, it is *compulsory / unsuitable*.
5 A person you can't count on is *reliable / unreliable*.
6 If something turns out a certain way, the results are *expected / unexpected*.

Exercise 6

Choose the best answer to complete the sentences.

1 I tried to make a doctor's appointment for tomorrow, but he's too busy to *follow me up / fit me in / rule me out*.
2 The presentation is *pulled off for / ruled out for / aimed at* teachers with little or no experience.
3 After an hour, the talk show host started to *set out / end up / wind up* the conversation.
4 Things didn't *turn out / wind up / follow up* the way I thought they would.
5 I've got lots of revision to do. I'd better *start on / set out / run into* my work.
6 How do you *count on / set out / go about* changing your password?

Exercise 7

Complete the sentences with the correct form of the phrasal verbs in the box.

| turn out | set out | set out | run into | go about | follow up |

1 The idea has been _____ by our researchers.
2 I'm not sure how to _____ setting up my own business.
3 We might _____ some problems later on.
4 Andrew _____ to establish himself as a journalist.
5 This will depend on how things _____.
6 In the journal, she _____ her theory in detail.

Exercise 8

Read the conversation. <u>Underline</u> all the phrasal verbs, then in your own words, explain what each one means below.

> **Chinedu:** How should we go about planning our wedding?
>
> **Stephanie:** Well, we could start on the guest list this afternoon.
>
> **Chinedu:** I think we should really try to line up a venue first.
>
> **Stephanie:** We can't rely on good weather, so let's rule out outdoor venues.
>
> **Chinedu:** That's true – we don't want to wind up getting married in the rain!
>
> **Stephanie:** Planning a wedding isn't easy. But I'm sure we'll pull it off!

1 _____   4 _____
2 _____   5 _____
3 _____   6 _____

Your turn!

Think of an event or activity you would like to organize. Use the phrasal verbs in this unit to talk about it. For example:

The event would be aimed at young people.

Discussions

agree with

If you agree with an action or suggestion, you approve of it.

You didn't ask anybody whether they agreed with what you were doing.

back down

If you back down, you start to accept someone else's opinion or demand, even though you do not want to.

Eventually he backed down on the question of pay.

NOTE   You can also use give in.

back up

If you back up a statement, you give evidence to prove that it is true or reasonable.

You need some statistics to back up your claim.

Supporters of this theory offer no evidence to back it up.

bring into

1 If you bring someone into an event or group, you ask them to take part in it or be part of it.

Greece has got to be brought into the talks.

2 If you bring a subject into a discussion or situation, you introduce it or start talking about it.

They always bring money into it.

come down to

If a problem, question, or situation comes down to a particular thing, that is the most important thing about it.

It all comes down to what sort of education you received.

give in

1 If you give in, you finally agree to do what someone wants you to do even though you do not want to do it.

He can say what he likes – I won't give in.

2 If you give in, you finally accept that someone else has defeated you and you stop competing.

All right, I give in – what's the answer?

go back on

If you go back on a promise, agreement, or statement, you do not do what you promised or agreed, or you say something which is the opposite of what you said earlier.

It wouldn't be fair to go back on all those promises.

go back to

If you go back to a point in a discussion or conversation, you start talking about it again.

Going back to what you said earlier, we simply don't have the budget for this.

go into

If you go into a particular subject, you describe it fully or in detail.

He went into the matter in some detail.

insist on

If you insist on something, you ask for it firmly and refuse to accept anything else.

He insisted on paying for the meal.

NOTE You can also use insist upon.

listen to

1 When you listen to someone or something, you give your attention to a sound or to what someone says.

You need to sit quietly and listen to the teacher.

2 If you listen to someone or to what someone says, you pay attention to them and let them influence you.

He never listened to his mother.

point out

1 If you point out an object or person, you tell someone that they are there or use your hand to show them.

Dino had pointed her out at the party.

They walked up the street, and she pointed out the café.

2 If you point something out, you give people an important piece of information that they did not know.

Critics were quick to point out the weaknesses in these arguments.

I pointed this fact out to him in the meeting.

stand by

If you stand by something, you continue to believe that it is correct or true.

I said I could do it and I stand by that.

NOTE You can also use abide by and adhere to. These are more formal.

NOTE The opposite of stand by is go back on.

talk into

If you talk someone into doing something, you persuade them to do it.

She talked me into taking a week's holiday.

NOTE The opposite of talk into is talk out of.

talk out of

If you talk someone out of doing something, you persuade them not to do it.

He tried to talk me out of buying such a big car.

win over

If you win someone over, you persuade them to support or agree with you or you make them like you. [mainly BRITISH]

I was completely won over by the courtesy and decency of the people.

His directness and obvious honesty were winning people over.

Exercise 1

Complete the sentences with the particles in the box.

down | by | into | out of | to | back on | out | down to

1 The government has refused to back _____ on this issue.
2 I think it comes _____ how much money you have.
3 He said he would stand _____ his comments even if it ended his political career.
4 'Did she say why she was going there?' – 'No, she didn't go _____ it.'
5 When I pointed this _____ to Adam, he got upset.
6 Is there anything I can say to talk you _____ it?
7 I should have listened _____ your advice.
8 Now you're going _____ what you told me earlier.

Exercise 2

Correct the phrasal verbs in these sentences.

1 I didn't want to go out after work, but my colleagues insisted in it.
2 The guide pointed up all the places of interest along the journey.
3 OK, I'll join the committee. I didn't want to, but you've managed to talk me over it!
4 She won the interviewers through with her excellent presentation.
5 Nobody agrees with the manager's decision, but he refuses to back up.
6 When it comes in to working overtime, everyone wants to make their opinions heard.
7 She had strong beliefs and always stood up her decisions.
8 I can't go back up my word.

Exercise 3

Match phrasal verbs 1–6 with definitions A–F.

1 agree with   A start talking about something again
2 back up   B give your attention to
3 insist on   C give evidence to prove something is true
4 go back to   D ask for something and refuse anything else
5 listen to   E show someone where something is (or give important information)
6 point out   F approve of something

Exercise 4

Decide if the following sentences are true (*T*) or false (*F*).

1 If you talk someone out of something, you persuade them not to do it. □
2 If you point something out, you persuade someone to do something. □
3 If you give in, you start talking about something. □
4 If you bring something into a discussion, you start talking about it. □
5 If you talk someone into something, you persuade them to do it. □
6 If you listen to someone, you pay attention to them. □

Exercise 5

Match sentence halves 1–8 with A–H to make complete sentences.

1 If you don't listen to all the arguments,   A to a point you made earlier.
2 It's no good trying to talk me out   B you won't be able to make a fair judgement.
3 We haven't got time to   C of my decision.
4 I'd like to just point out   D go into the matter more thoroughly at the moment.
5 I know you want me to change my mind   E that we all agreed on this two weeks ago.
6 I just want to go back   F but I'm not going to give in.
7 A true friend would never   G her earlier comments.
8 She said she stands by   H go back on a promise.

Exercise 6

Complete the sentences with the correct form of the phrasal verbs in the box.

| talk ... into | talk ... out of | point out | listen to | go into | back ... up |

1 The tour guide _____ various landmarks to us.
2 Don't _____ anyone who tells you anything different.
3 I really don't want to _____ it right now.
4 Gary _____ his argument _____ with various examples.
5 I don't want her to go, so I'm going to try to _____ her _____ it.
6 I decided to apply for the job after my boss _____ me _____ doing it.

Exercise 7

Read the discussion about a newspaper article. <u>Underline</u> all the phrasal verbs, then answer the questions which follow.

Josh: I agree with most of the points the author makes, but not all of them.

Ryan: He didn't win me over with his argument at all. He just didn't back up any of his claims with facts or research.

Josh: But if you listen to what he said about how technology has changed society, you have to agree with him.

Ryan: No, for me it all comes down to money – that's what really matters.

1 Does Josh agree with all the points made by the author?
2 Does Ryan agree with any of the points made in the article?
3 What does Ryan think the author failed to do?
4 On what issue does Josh agree with the author?
5 What is the most important issue for Ryan?

Exercise 8

Make these sentences less formal. Replace the <u>underlined</u> verbs with the phrasal verbs in the box.

| back up | bring ... into | stand by | gave in | go into | insisted on | listening to |

1 We finally <u>surrendered</u> to their demands.
2 Can you <u>support</u> your argument with any examples?
3 I'd rather not <u>discuss</u> this here.
4 Hannah always <u>insisted upon</u> only the best restaurants.
5 Are you actually <u>paying attention to</u> me?
6 I'd like to <u>introduce</u> a new topic <u>into</u> the debate.
7 We still <u>abide by</u> our earlier decision to fire him.

Your turn!

Read an article about a subject you find interesting in a newspaper, journal or online. Use the phrasal verbs in this unit to talk about your opinions on the subject. For example:

I found it interesting that the author went into her experiences in detail.

Advice or warnings

come on

1. You say come on to someone when you want to encourage them.

   Come on, you're doing fine. Lean on me and I'll get you home.

2. You say come on to someone when you want them to come somewhere more quickly.

   Come on, Sophie, we're going to be late.

   NOTE   You can also use come along.

give up

If you give up or give up something, you stop doing an activity that you often used to do.

Philip has given up smoking.

I used to jog but I gave it up because it was hurting my knees.

I used to smoke, but I gave up a couple of years ago.

keep from

1. keep someone from doing something, or keep something from happening means to stop them doing it or stop something from happening.

   Dad tried to keep me from going.

   We tied up the bags to keep the rubbish from falling out.

2. If you keep from doing something, you manage to stop yourself doing it, but it is difficult.

   Did you manage to keep from telling the secret?

keep out

1. To keep someone or something out means to stop them from entering a place or being there.

   There is a guard dog to keep out intruders.

   The net keeps mosquitoes and other insects out.

2. If a sign says Keep Out, it is warning you not to go onto that piece of land.

   'Private property. Keep out.'

look down

If you look down, you lower your eyes to see what is below.

He paused on the narrow ledge and looked down.

look out

You say look out to warn someone about something that you have noticed, especially danger.

'Look out,' I said. 'There's someone coming.'

NOTE   You can also use watch out.

mess up

If you mess something up, you spoil it or do it badly.

One mistake will mess up the whole project.

You've messed the printing up – it's printed on the same side twice.

pull over

1. When a vehicle or driver pulls over, they move closer to the side of the road, and stop.

   Drivers need safe places to pull over when feeling tired.

2. If the police pull a car or driver over, they signal to the driver to drive the car to the side of the road and stop.

   We saw a police car pulling over a lorry.

   A police car pulled them over.

run to

If you run to someone, you go to them for help, advice or protection.

We must learn to trust our own intuition and judgment, and not always run to the experts.

settle down

If people settle down or if you settle them down, they become calm or quiet.

Settle down, children. You're making too much noise.

It took the teacher several minutes to settle the class down.

NOTE   You can also use calm down.

step up

If you step up something, you increase its speed, amount, or intensity.

You're going too slowly. Step up the pace a little.

The candidate is stepping his campaign up as the election approaches.

stick to

1. If you stick to something, you continue to do what you have decided or what is expected.

   The diet won't work unless you stick to it.

   NOTE   You can also use keep to.

2. If you stick to something or someone, you stay close to them.

   It's best to stick to well-lit roads.

3. If you stick to a subject, you talk only about it, and not about anything else.

   Don't give your opinions, just stick to the facts.

   NOTE   You can also use keep to.

stick with

1. If you stick with something, you continue to use it or do it, rather than changing.

   Should they stick with the business or try to start something else?

   NOTE   You can also use stick at and stick to.

2. If you stick with someone, you stay close to them.

   Stick with me and you'll be okay, don't you worry.

try for

If you try for something, you make an effort to get it or achieve it.

The school advised me to try for Oxford University.

turn to

If you turn to someone, you ask them for help or advice.

I have no other friend to turn to.

watch out

If you tell someone to watch out, you are warning them to be careful because something unpleasant might happen to them.

If you don't watch out, he might cause trouble for you.

NOTE   You can also use look out.

Exercise 1

Complete the sentences with the verbs in the box.

watch | stuck | give | pull | settle | messed | keep | come

1 _____ on, Mike, you can do it!
2 Good sunglasses will help to _____ the sun out of your eyes.
3 We had been driving for hours so decided to _____ over and have a rest.
4 When they went walking in the mountains, they _____ to the paths.
5 There are bears in these woods, so you'd better _____ out.
6 I think I might have _____ up my exams.
7 Please _____ down and be quiet!
8 His doctor advised him to _____ up drinking coffee.

Exercise 2

Complete the sentences. Choose the correct particles.

1 We've built a wall around the vegetable garden to keep *out / from / down* animals.
2 I know it's difficult to learn a language, but if you stick *to / up / with* it, it'll get easier.
3 We're taking the cable car to the top of the mountain. If you're afraid of heights, don't look *in / down / over*!
4 He always runs *in / for / to* his best friends for advice.
5 I'm sorry. I think I messed *up / out / at* my presentation. I showed the slides in the wrong order.
6 You're really good at athletics, you know. Why don't you try *out / on / for* the team?

Exercise 3

Match phrasal verbs 1–6 with definitions A–F.

1 Cut down on sugar and step up your intake of fresh foods.   A warning to tell someone to be careful
2 Watch out! There's a waterfall ahead.   B continue to do something
3 Their doctor said they could try for a baby.   C talk only about something
4 I think we should stick to the point.   D increase the amount of something
5 I know you find this difficult, but stick with it.   E go to someone for help or advice
6 He always runs to her whenever things go wrong.   F make an effort to achieve something

Exercise 4

Match sentence halves 1–6 with A–F to make complete sentences.

1 I was so cold I couldn't   A he told me to look out.
2 In times of difficulty you can   B be okay.
3 As he cycled towards me   C and don't look down!
4 I don't want to mess up   D keep from shivering.
5 Come on, Kara, it'll   E always turn to your parents.
6 My advice is keep climbing   F my life again.

Exercise 5

Complete these road signs with the correct particles in the box.

OUT | OUT | OUT | OVER | OVER | TO

1 IF YOU'RE TIRED, PULL _____
2 FALLING ROCKS – LOOK _____!
3 KEEP _____ – ROAD CLOSED
4 STICK _____ LOW SPEEDS FOR NEXT 20 MILES
5 PULL _____ TO ALLOW AMBULANCES THROUGH
6 WATCH _____: ANIMALS CROSSING

Exercise 6

Replace the <u>underlined</u> verbs with a phrasal verb from the box with the same meaning.

watch out | given up | stick to | mess up | keep to | settle ... down | keep from | come on

1 <u>Come along</u>, we don't want to be late for the film!
2 '<u>Look out</u>!' somebody shouted, as the truck started to roll toward the sea.
3 Start a new exercise regime and this time <u>stick to</u> it.
4 I can't <u>resist</u> mentioning my favourite scene in the film.
5 Of course we will <u>adhere to</u> our policy.
6 I don't want to <u>spoil</u> my chances.
7 Read your child a story to <u>calm</u> her <u>down</u>.
8 Gemma has <u>stopped</u> taking sugar in her tea.

Exercise 7

Complete the sentences with the correct forms of phrasal verbs from this unit.

1 I was driving too fast, and the police _____ me _____ and took my details.
2 A long distance runner needs to _____ the speed just before the finishing line.
3 When I was younger, I couldn't _____ biting my nails. Luckily I've grown out of that habit now.
4 There's a huge crowd of people at the concert, so in order not to get lost, _____ me.
5 _____, hurry up! We're going to be late!

Exercise 8

Read the question and answer from an advice website. <u>Underline</u> all the phrasal verbs, then decide if the sentences that follow are true (*T*) or false (*F*).

Dear Ali,

My parents have always encouraged me to try for medical school, but I think I may have messed up the entrance exam. I just don't know who to turn to for help or what to do next. Can you help?

Jack

Dear Jack,

Don't let one failure keep you from doing what you want to do. If going to medical school is your dream, then you should stick with it. Step up your efforts to make sure you get a place in another school. You can do it!

Ali

1 Jack's parents wanted him to go to medical school. ☐
2 Jack has passed the entrance exam. ☐
3 Jack doesn't know who to ask for help. ☐
4 Ali tells Jack not to go to medical school. ☐
5 Ali encourages Jack to follow his dreams. ☐
6 Ali advises Jack to try for other schools. ☐

Your turn!

Look for a website that gives advice on a subject that interests you. Can you find any examples of the phrasal verbs in this unit?

Come on! You can't stay there forever.

Thinking and knowing

bring back

If something brings back an event or memory from your past, it makes you think about it.

The death of a friend can bring back memories of childhood loss.

These photos bring it all back.

come back

If something that you had forgotten comes back, you remember it, often quite suddenly.

I hadn't thought about it for years and then it all came back to me when I saw him in the street.

figure out

1. If you figure out the solution to a problem, the answer to a question, or the reason for something, you work it out and understand it. [INFORMAL]

I've figured out what the trouble is.

Nancy couldn't figure it out.

2. If you figure someone out, you understand why they behave in the way they do. [INFORMAL]

He won't let anyone help him. I just can't figure him out.

go back

1. If something goes back to a particular time in the past, it has existed since that time.

These customs go back a long way.

NOTE   You can also use date back.

2. If you go back, you consider things that happened at a time in the past.

To trace its origins, we have to go back some thirty million years.

go by

If a period of time goes by, it passes.

Eight years went by.

hear about

If you hear about something or someone or hear something about them, you get news or information about them.

They heard about a new restaurant that was opening in town.

I've heard lots of good things about him.

hear of

1. If you hear of something, you find out something about it or find out that it exists for the first time.

How did you first hear of his work?

2. If you have heard of someone or something, you are aware that they exist.

I have never heard of the writer they are talking about.

know about

If you know about a subject, you have studied it and understand part or all of it.

You ought to ask John, he knows about photography.

look back

If you look back, you think about something that happened in the past.

The past always seems better when you look back on it.

pass on

1. If you pass something on, you give or tell it to someone else.

   If you hear any tips, do pass them on.

   I could pass on a message if you like.

2. If things such as stories, traditions, or money are passed on, or you pass them on, they are taught or given to someone who belongs to a younger generation.

   Skills such as this should be passed on.

   They pass on their traditions through storytelling.

   NOTE   You can also use hand down.

remind of

1. If you remind someone of something, you tell them about it so that they remember it.

   May I remind you of something you said earlier?

2. If one person or thing reminds you of another, they make you think of the other person or thing, because they are similar in some way.

   You remind me of my friend Baxter.

stick in

If something sticks in your mind or memory, you continue to remember it very clearly.

Some things stick in your memory for ever.

think of

1. If you can think of something or someone, you know them and can therefore suggest them to other people.

   Can you think of anyone who could help us?

2. If you think of an idea, you create it.

   I began to think of new methods.

3. If you think of doing something, you consider the possibility of doing it.

   I'm thinking of buying him a present.

work out

1. If you work out the answer to a mathematical problem, you calculate it.

   I've worked it out, and it's 3,171.875 tons.

   The weekly rate is worked out by dividing by 52.

2. If something works out at a particular amount, it is found to be that amount after all the calculations have been made.

   The cost of the fuel worked out to be higher than they had expected.

3. If you work out a solution or a plan, you think about it carefully and find a solution or decide what to do.

   We should try to work out the best ways to help these young people.

   I've been trying to find a solution and I think I've finally worked it out.

4. If you manage to work out something that seems strange, you think about it and manage to understand it.

   I'm trying to work out what's wrong.

   I'm not sure what's missing yet, but I'll work it out.

   NOTE   You can also use figure out.

Exercise 1

Match the verbs with the particles in the box to make phrasal verbs from this unit.

of | back | about | out

1 bring / come / go / look
2 hear / remind / think
3 figure / work
4 hear / know

Exercise 2

Complete the sentences. Choose the correct particles.

1 I used a map to figure *about / out / over* the best route.
2 Ellie doesn't know anything *about / out / over* me.
3 The girl reminded me *back / in / of* my own daughter.
4 Have you ever thought *over / of / into* moving abroad?
5 I always use a calculator to work it *out / about / into*.
6 Can you pass *by / of / on* a message for me?
7 Several months went *by / over / with* before we saw each other again.
8 This painting dates *in / back / over* to the sixteenth century.

Exercise 3

Correct the phrasal verbs in these sentences.

1 Have you heard anything more with the bus strike next weekend?
2 It's a tradition that goes by to the 17th century.
3 I can't work at how to switch on this machine.
4 What advice will you pass back to your children one day?
5 As soon as I hear that music, memories come over to me.
6 I'll never forget it. It's something that will always stick up my mind.
7 He looks over on his school days very fondly.
8 I'm thinking on starting my own business.

Exercise 4

Match sentence halves 1–6 with A–F to make complete definitions.

1 If something brings
2 If a memory comes
3 If you think of doing
4 If you work something
5 If you look back, you think
6 If you know about something,

A about something in the past.
B you have studied it and understand it.
C back a memory, it makes you think about it.
D out, you manage to understand it.
E something, you consider the possibility of doing it.
F back, you remember it suddenly.

Exercise 5

Decide if the following sentences are true (*T*) or false (*F*).

1 Date back means the same as go back. ☐
2 Hear about means the same as remind of. ☐
3 Work out means the same as figure out. ☐
4 Pass on means the same as hand down. ☐
5 Look back means the same as come back. ☐
6 Stick in means the same as hear of. ☐
7 Bring back means the same as date back. ☐
8 Think of means the same as go by. ☐

Exercise 6

Replace the <u>underlined</u> words and phrases with the phrasal verbs in the box.

| figure out | know much about | go back | brings back memories of | go by | think of |

1 The smell of suntan oil always <u>makes me remember</u> summer holidays.
2 I can't <u>find the solution to</u> this problem.
3 We can never <u>return</u> to the past.
4 Can you <u>suggest</u> a capital city that begins with D?
5 Do you <u>have any information about</u> Antarctica?
6 I see my friends from school less and less often, as the years <u>pass by</u>.

Exercise 7

Complete the sentences with the phrasal verbs in the box.

| brought back | goes by | heard of | handed down | passed on | stuck in | come back | dates back |

1 As time _____, I feel less angry about it.
2 His unusual bright yellow coat had _____ her mind.
3 Leon's father had _____ the stories to him.
4 I have never _____ this singer.
5 I can't remember her name, but I'm sure it'll _____ to me.
6 Talking about home _____ sad memories for Carla.
7 The first scientific study _____ to the early 1960s.
8 The story had been _____ from generation to generation in his family.

Exercise 8

Read the extract from Kimberly's cookery blog. <u>Underline</u> all the phrasal verbs, then match them with the correct definitions 1–6.

> I love the smell of spicy chicken cooking because it reminds me of Jamaica. I live in the UK now, but my love of Jamaican food goes back to my childhood in Jamaica. The thing that sticks in my memory is my mother cooking this for the whole family every weekend. Several years have gone by since I moved to the UK, so I want to pass on my cooking skills to my children. I want them to know more about Jamaican culture.

1 has existed since
2 makes me think about
3 give or teach
4 understand more regarding
5 continues clearly in
6 passed

Your turn!

What memories do you have of your childhood?
Use the phrasal verbs in this unit to talk about
what you remember. For example:

I look back on it as a wonderful time.

10

Feelings

calm down

1. If you calm down or if someone or something calms you down, you become less upset, excited, or angry.

   'Please, Mrs Green,' said Brandon. 'Calm down. Let me explain'.

   One of the speakers tried to calm the crowd down.

   'I wouldn't like to see you really lose your temper,' he remarked, trying to calm down the man.

2. If a situation calms down or if you calm it down, the people involved in it become less upset, excited or angry.

   He told me that things appeared to be calming down a bit.

   Dad managed to calm things down.

   NOTE   You can also use settle down.

care for

1. If you care for someone or something, you look after them and keep them in a good state or condition.

   She has to care for her elderly parents.

2. If you care for someone, you love them.

   At last she had found a man that she cared for and who cared for her.

cheer up

When you cheer up or when someone or something cheers you up, you stop feeling sad and become happier.

He cheered up a little at the prospect of dinner.

I took some cake into work to try to cheer up my colleagues.

She bought strawberries to cheer herself up.

deal with

If you deal with a negative emotion or a situation that causes negative emotions, you manage to control your feelings and continue your normal life.

She saw a psychiatrist who used hypnotism to help her deal with her fear.

NOTE   You can also use cope with.

face up to

If you face up to a difficult situation, you accept it and deal with it.

We have to face up to the fact that this relationship isn't going to work.

get over

1. If you get over an illness or another unpleasant experience, you recover from it.

   He's had a shock but he's getting over it.

2. If you get over a problem or difficulty, you find a way of dealing with it.

   We could get over the problem by hiring more staff.

get to

If an experience gets to you, it upsets or annoys you. [INFORMAL]

She can be quite rude sometimes but don't let it get to you.

go through

If you go through an event or period of time, especially an unpleasant one, you experience it.

She's going through a busy period in her life.

hope for

If you hope for something, you want it and expect to have it.

The team is hoping for a big win today.

let down

If someone or something lets you down, they fail to do something that you expected or wanted them to do.

He would never let a friend down.

I feel guilty about letting down my parents.

look forward to

If you look forward to something, you are happy it is going to happen because you expect to enjoy it.

I was not looking forward to my meeting with the manager.

We are really looking forward to our skiing holiday.

open up

If someone opens up, they start to relax and talk about personal things.

It can be hard to get teenagers to open up and talk to their parents.

play on

If you play on people's feelings, attitudes, or weaknesses, you deliberately use them in order to achieve what you want.

He played on their prejudices and their fears.

Try to find your opponent's weaknesses and play on them relentlessly.

NOTE   You can also use play upon.

relate to

1 If you can relate to other people, you can understand how they feel and communicate with them easily.

Children need to learn to relate to other children.

2 If you relate to something, you understand it because you have had a similar experience or emotion or have a similar opinion.

These people have a way of looking at the world that most of us find hard to relate to.

Exercise 1

Match verbs 1–4 with particles A–D to make phrasal verbs from this unit.

1 cheer / open   **A** for
2 calm / let   **B** up
3 care / hope   **C** to
4 relate / get   **D** down

Exercise 2

Choose the best answer to complete the sentences.

1 It took her a long time to *go through / get over / care for* the loss of her pet cat.
2 We're all *hoping for / relating to / opening up to* a solution to the problem.
3 I don't understand it. It's something I just can't *get to / play on / relate to*.
4 Are you *cheering up / calming down / looking forward to* your trip?
5 A good teacher is able to *let down / calm down / go through* a class of noisy, excitable children.
6 I know it's annoying, but try not to let it *cheer you up / open you up / get to you*.
7 You should *open up / calm down / look forward* to her and talk about how you feel.
8 She did not want to *calm down / cheer up / let down* her boss, so she agreed to work more overtime.

Exercise 3

Complete the sentences with the particles in the box.

up to	to	for	over	up	with	on	down

1 Without him I could not possibly have faced _____ all my fears and difficulties.
2 Cerys always does a good job. She never lets me _____.
3 The family are dealing _____ their loss and ask that their privacy is respected.
4 Chad booked a holiday to cheer himself _____.
5 She always likes to have something to look forward _____.
6 It took a long time for her parents to get _____ the shock.
7 He played _____ the fact that people felt sorry for him.
8 She really cared _____ him.

Exercise 4

Match sentence halves 1–6 with A–F to make complete sentences.

1 A police officer tried to   **A** permanent relationship with John.
2 She lives with a nurse   **B** what she said about music.
3 His rude behaviour was really starting   **C** to get to me.
4 James played   **D** on Daphne's guilt.
5 I could relate to   **E** calm her down.
6 Anya was hoping for a more   **F** who cares for her.

Exercise 5

Match phrasal verbs 1–6 with definitions A–F.

1 Please just calm down!   **A** upset or annoy
2 The company really let us down, so I won't use them   **B** stop (him) feeling sad and make (him) become happier
    again.   **C** happy (something) is going to happen because we
3 He could easily relate to her situation.   expect to enjoy it
4 We're really looking forward to the weekend.   **D** failed to do something (I) expected
5 I don't know what I can do to cheer him up.   **E** become less upset, excited, or angry
6 Don't let these silly remarks get to you.   **F** understand (something) because he has had a
                                              similar experience

Exercise 6

Replace the <u>underlined</u> verbs with a phrasal verb from the box with the same meaning.

plays on | got over | gone through | deal with | calmed down

1 A year after the accident, things have <u>settled down</u> again.
2 Mohammed now finds it easier to <u>cope with</u> his workload.
3 She still hasn't <u>recovered from</u> the shock.
4 The news story simply <u>plays upon</u> existing fears.
5 The family have <u>undergone</u> a terrible trauma.

Exercise 7

Complete the sentences with the correct form of the phrasal verbs in the box.

care for | face up to | get over | go through | hope for | open up

1 After a few hours he began to _____ about his problems.
2 He used to _____ the children while she was away.
3 The best we can _____ is to get at least some of our money back.
4 They have _____ such a hard time lately.
5 Sooner or later you have to _____ the truth.
6 He never _____ the death of his wife.

Exercise 8

Read the email. <u>Underline</u> all the phrasal verbs, then in your own words, explain what each one means.

> Hi Liam
>
> How are you? I'm okay. I had a car accident last weekend. I was really shocked when it happened but I've calmed down now and am getting over it. However, I may have to face up to the fact that the accident was my fault. I'm sure you can relate to all this after your car accident last year. Anyway, I'm really looking forward to seeing you next weekend as I need something to cheer me up!
>
> See you soon,
>
> Emily

1 _____   4 _____
2 _____   5 _____
3 _____   6 _____

Your turn!

Have you ever been in a difficult situation? Use the phrasal verbs in this unit to talk about how it made you feel. For example:

I felt so bad about letting down my friends.

It helps him **deal with** the stress.

11

Attitudes

believe in

[1] If you believe in things such as fairies or miracles, you are sure that they really exist or happen.

Do you believe in ghosts?

[2] If you believe in an idea or policy, you support it because you think it is right.

He's very conservative and believes in personal responsibility.

[3] If you believe in someone, you have confidence in them and think that they will be successful.

I won't give up on you, because I believe in you.

NOTE   You can also use have confidence in.

go for

[1] If you go for a particular thing, you choose it or try to achieve it.

They urged the Chancellor to go for the first option.

[2] If you go for someone or something, you like them very much.

I don't really go for that kind of food.

live up to

If someone or something lives up to what is expected, they are as good as they were expected to be.

The film didn't live up to my expectations.

NOTE   You can also use match up to.

look at

If you look at a situation in a particular way, you judge it or consider it in that way.

I tend to look at things in a very different way from my parents.

look up to

If you look up to someone, you respect and admire them.

She looks up to her father.

object to

If you object to something, you do not like it or approve of it.

Local residents have objected to the plan.

oppose to

If you are opposed to something, you disagree with it or disapprove of it.

We are opposed to plans to build more houses here.

pick on

If you pick on someone, you treat them badly or in an unfair way, often repeatedly.

Maria had complained that the teacher was picking on her.

NOTE You can also use get at.

put down

If you put someone down, you criticize them and make them feel stupid.

Another thing that upsets me is the way Alex tries to put me down in public.

I hate the way she puts down people in meetings.

put off

To put someone off something or someone means to make them not want to do something or not like something or someone.

The country's high prices have put off many tourists.

The disgusting smell put me off my breakfast.

put up with

If you put up with something or someone, you accept them, even though you do not like them.

Don't put up with Howard´s bad behaviour.

see as

If you see someone or something as a particular thing, you believe that they are that thing or have that quality.

He saw her as the perfect woman.

settle for

If you settle for something, you choose or accept it even though it is not what you really want.

Don't settle for second best.

show off

If you show off, you try to impress people by showing them what you can do or telling them what you have done, usually in a way that is annoying.

He's always showing off about how important his job is.

stand for

The things that someone stands for are the ideas or values that they support or represent.

Our organization has always stood for individual liberty.

walk out

If you walk out, you leave a place or a performance as a way of showing that you are angry or that you do not like something.

Many of the audience walked out through boredom.

Exercise 1

Match verbs 1–4 with particles A–D to make phrasal verbs from this unit.

1 look / live   A off
2 put / show   B up to
3 object / oppose   C for
4 stand / go   D to

Exercise 2

Match phrasal verbs 1–6 with definitions A–F.

1 put up with   A be as good as expected
2 go for   B respect and admire someone
3 oppose to   C accept something, even though you do not like it
4 live up to   D leave a place to show you are angry or do not like something
5 walk out   E disagree with or disapprove of something
6 look up to   F choose or try to achieve something

Exercise 3

Answer the questions.

1 Would a person be pleased or upset if you picked on him/her?
2 Is it usually considered positive or negative to show off?
3 If you put up with someone, do you accept that person or not?
4 If you settle for something, is it usually exactly what you want, or not quite what you want?
5 If you stand for an idea, do you support that idea or not?
6 If you put someone down, are you praising or criticising that person?

Exercise 4

Complete the sentences. Choose the correct particles.

1 She was always putting him *down / with / at*.
2 Don't be put *in / off / at* by the high prices.
3 He's a religious man; he believes *on / at / in* God.
4 Veronica strongly objected *to / out / up* his remarks.
5 Why should you settle *for / to / under* anything less?
6 He hoped he could live *on to / in to / up to* their expectations.
7 He wasn't brave enough to stand *on to / up to / in to* her.
8 She didn't really go *up / to / for* adventure holidays – she preferred to relax.

Exercise 5

Complete the sentences with the phrasal verbs in the box.

| match up to | walked out | showing off | picked on | look at | sees ... as | settle for | objected to |

1 Did we succeed? It all depends how you _____ it.
2 She _____ him reading her text messages.
3 The other girls _____ her at school.
4 The president was furious and _____ of the conference.
5 If there's no apple juice I'll _____ orange juice.
6 The boys were _____ with their skateboards.
7 She _____ saving money _____ a good thing.
8 The new car didn't really _____ his expectations.

Exercise 6

Make these sentences less formal. Replace the <u>underlined</u> verbs with the phrasal verbs in the box.

believe in | put up with | going for | stands for | seen ... as | looks at

1 Helena wasn't sure she could <u>endure</u> much more of this.
2 She had always <u>considered</u> him <u>as</u> a good friend.
3 Kim <u>views</u> life as an adventure.
4 He does not <u>support</u> cruelty of any kind.
5 This goes against everything our brand <u>represents</u>.
6 I always end up <u>choosing</u> the chocolate milkshake.

Exercise 7

Correct the phrasal verbs in these sentences.

1 Jane did not agree with what the company stood off.
2 We see business on being closely linked to education.
3 I'm not opposed in the idea of nuclear power.
4 It isn't always easy to live down to such high standards.
5 We just ignore Kevin when he shows on.
6 I usually go on the cheapest option.
7 Jay was always getting out his little brother.
8 He walked at after a furious argument.

Exercise 8

Read Viktor's comment about his teacher. <u>Underline</u> all the phrasal verbs, then answer the questions.

I look up to my science teacher. He never picks on anyone or puts people down, even though he often has to put up with some badly behaved students. We have our first science exam next month. I'm not trying to show off, but he tells me I am a strong student and that he believes in me.

1 Does Viktor admire his science teacher?
2 Does Viktor's teacher treat some of the students badly?
3 Do all the students behave well?
4 What will happen next month?
5 What is Viktor trying not to do?
6 Does Viktor's teacher have confidence in him?

Your turn!

Think of someone or something you approve or disapprove of. Use the phrasal verbs in this unit to talk about your views on them. For example:

I strongly object to testing on animals.

I believe in the importance of free education.

The new player **lived up to** the team's expectations.

12

Relationships

break down

When an arrangement, relationship or discussion breaks down, it fails because of a problem or disagreement.

It is always very sad when a marriage breaks down.

depend on

1. If you depend on someone or something, you need them in order to be able to survive physically, financially, or emotionally.

   I feel that he depends on me too much for a social life.

   NOTE   You can also use depend upon and rely on.

2. If you can depend on someone or something, you know that you can trust them to do something.

   I knew I could depend on you.

   NOTE   You can also use depend upon and rely on.

do with

1. If someone has something to do with something else, they are involved in doing it or making it happen.

   I suspect she had something to do with Tom's disappearance.

2. If something is nothing to do with or has nothing to do with someone, that person has no reason to know about it or become involved with it.

   What I do in my free time is nothing to do with him.

   Just forget about it. It has nothing to do with you.

3. If one thing is to do with or has to do with something else, the two things are related in some way.

   So what was the discussion about? Was it to do with the new project?

   I don't know what he does exactly but it has to do with computers.

fall apart

If an organization, activity, system or relationship falls apart, it fails or ends.

Their marriage began to fall apart.

fall for

If you fall for someone or something, you start to love them or like them very much.

He fell for her the moment he first saw her.

fall out

If people fall out, they have an argument and are no longer friendly.

I've fallen out with certain members of the band.

finish with

1 If you finish with someone or something, or are finished with them, you stop dealing with them or end your involvement with them.

I haven't finished with you yet.

He decided he was finished with marriage.

2 If you finish with someone, you end your romantic relationship with them. [BRITISH]

We were together for three months but it was not a good relationship and I finished with him.

get on

If two people get on, they have a friendly relationship. [mainly BRITISH]

Mark and Jason don't get on.

NOTE   You can also use get along.

get together

If two people get together, they start a romantic relationship. [INFORMAL]

Lara and Pete got together after meeting at Ann's party.

go out

If two people go out, they have a romantic relationship with each other.

My parents wouldn't let me go out with boys.

make up

If two people make up, they become friends again after they have had an argument.

The two actors have now made up after a very public disagreement.

make up for

If you make up for something, you do something to show that you are sorry or to make someone less unhappy.

She tried to make up for her rudeness earlier by being extra nice to me.

rely on

1 To rely on something or someone means to need them in order to survive or be successful.

She is forced to rely on her mother's money.

NOTE   You can also use rely upon and depend on.

2 If you can rely on someone or something to work or behave in a particular way, you trust them to do this.

You can always rely on him to be polite and do the right thing.

NOTE   You can also use rely upon.

NOTE   You can also use count on. This is more informal.

settle down

If someone settles down, they start living in one place, often with a partner, and intend to stay there for a long time.

Your parents want you to get a job and settle down.

walk out

If you walk out, you leave the person or people you live with and do not come back.

His father walked out when he was a baby.

Exercise 1

Match phrasal verbs 1–6 with definitions A–F.

1 I can depend on Terry to get the job done quickly.
2 We had our differences but we've made up now.
3 Kate and Brandon got together last summer.
4 She finished with him last week.
5 When we were younger, we used to fall out all the time.
6 Their relationship began to fall apart after a few years.

A become friends again after an argument
B end a romantic relationship with someone
C have an argument or stop being friendly with someone
D know you can trust someone
E something fails or ends
F start a romantic relationship with someone

Exercise 2

Complete the sentences. Choose the correct particles.

1 Talks between the two countries broke *out / down / for* last year.
2 She's so pretty – I fell *out / for / off* her straight away.
3 The couple started going *out / for / on* together six months ago.
4 It has nothing to do *out / with / on* her age.
5 Sorry I'm so late! Let me buy you dinner to make *in for / up for / on for* it.
6 After five years of difficulties, Keren decided to walk *out / for / up*.

Exercise 3

Match sentence halves 1–6 with A–F to make complete sentences.

1 We didn't use like each other at all, but now
2 I'm sorry you had an argument with Peter. I hope
3 She wants to travel around the world
4 I can't believe they're going out –
5 It was nice seeing you again;
6 Laura always seems to

A before she gets married and settles down.
B fall for the wrong type of man.
C they are so different.
D we get on really well.
E we must get together more often.
F you two make up again.

Exercise 4

Complete the sentences with the phrasal verbs in the box.

depends on	do with	fall out	get on	going out	settling down

1 The printer is broken. Did you have anything to _____ it?
2 We're thinking about _____ and starting a family.
3 She _____ her mother and father too much.
4 Hardeep and Sunita are a great couple, they really _____ well.
5 When did you two start _____ together?
6 I don't want us to _____ over something so stupid.

Exercise 5

Match comments 1–8 with the correct replies A–H.

1 Their friendship broke down because of a misunderstanding.
2 Jane is always falling for the wrong type of guy.
3 We got together a few weeks ago.
4 You seem to be getting on well with Charlie.
5 After days of arguing, they've finally made up.
6 I hope she finds someone nice to settle down with.
7 Dean sent her some flowers to make up for missing the party.
8 She isn't sure whether to finish with him or not.

A Yes, he's a really friendly guy.
B That was really nice of him!
C Well, I think she should definitely end it with him.
D I know. Apparently they haven't spoken to each other for two years.
E You're right about her. She really needs to find someone decent.
F Me too. She's been single for a long time.
G I see. So you haven't been together long then.
H I'm glad. It was silly of them to quarrel over nothing.

Exercise 6

Replace the <u>underlined</u> verbs with a phrasal verb from the box with the same meaning.

| depends upon | going out | get on | falling apart | count on |

1 He always <u>relies on</u> Olivia to pay for things.
2 I <u>get along</u> great with my wife's friends.
3 Selena and I started <u>dating</u> about four months ago.
4 I can always <u>rely on</u> her to say the right thing.
5 We tried counselling to stop our marriage <u>collapsing</u>.

Exercise 7

Correct the phrasal verbs in these sentences.

1 Sandra is a person you can always depend about to get things done in time.
2 He left the company after he fell down with his manager about salary.
3 You don't have to tell anyone what happened. It has nothing to do for them.
4 I'm sorry. I really want to make down with you.
5 He's very good looking. She fell about him as soon as she met him.
6 Don't walk away in the middle of an argument! I haven't finished off you yet.

Exercise 8

Read the magazine interview. <u>Underline</u> all the phrasal verbs, then decide if the sentences that follow are true (*T*) or false (*F*).

> Andrew and I first got together six years ago when we met on holiday. The fact that he's rich has nothing to do with why I fell for him. We just got along so well together, even though he's a lot older than me. What I love about Andrew is that I can rely on him to take care of me. But I don't depend on his money. I have always had plenty of my own!

1 Tara and Andrew started their relationship four years ago. ☐
2 Tara started to love him because he's rich. ☐
3 Andrew is younger than Tara. ☐
4 They have a friendly relationship, despite Andrew's age. ☐
5 Tara can trust Andrew to take care of her. ☐
6 Tara needs Andrew's money. ☐

Your turn!

Think about the relationships you have in your life.
Use the phrasal verbs in this unit to talk about them.
For example:

I get on well with my friend, Angelo.

When they first met they didn't **get on** at all.

Socializing and leisure time

call for

If you call for someone or something, you go to the building where they are, to collect them.

I'll call for you about eight.

call on

If you call on someone, you visit them for a short time.

Shall we call on Charlotte since we're so near?

catch up

If you catch up, you talk to a friend, finding out what has happened in his or her life since you last met.

It would be really nice to catch up over a cup of coffee sometime.

come along

If someone comes along, they go somewhere with you or go to the same place as you.

We're going out for dinner. Why don't you come along with us?

come out

If someone comes out, they go somewhere with someone socially.

Would you like to come out with us to the cinema?

come over

1 When someone comes over, they move across a room or other place towards you.

The waiter came over and put her drink down in front of her.

2 When someone comes over, they visit your house to see you for a short time.

Come over and have lunch with us tomorrow.

NOTE   You can also use come around.

drop in

To drop in means to visit someone informally, usually without having arranged the visit.

I thought I'd just drop in and see how you were.

NOTE   You can also use drop by and drop round.

NOTE   You can also use pop in. This is a more informal British form.

eat out

When you eat out, you have a meal at a restaurant instead of at home.

Do you eat out a lot in London?

NOTE   The opposite of eat out is eat in.

get in

1 When a person or a vehicle gets in, they arrive at a place where people are expecting them to be.

I'll tell him you called when he gets in.

2 If you get in, you succeed in entering a building.

We went to a museum and it cost ten euros to get in.

get together

When people get together, or when someone gets people together, two or more people meet in order to discuss something or to spend time with each other.

We should all get together and go out for a drink.

He got a bunch of people together who wanted to help out.

go out

When you go out, you leave your house and go somewhere else.

I thought we could go out somewhere for a picnic.

NOTE   The opposite of go out is stay in.

go over

If you go over, you go to someone's house and visit them for a short time.

There was a phone message from Jeremy, asking me to go over the next evening.

Can we go over to Ella's today?

NOTE   You can also use go round.

hang out

If you hang out somewhere or hang out, you spend a lot of time in a place, often not doing very much. [INFORMAL]

I don't hang out at the park any more.

Shall we go to town and just hang out?

put off

1 If you put off something, you delay it or arrange to do it at a later time than planned.

She used tiredness as an excuse to put off things she didn't want to do.

I know I've got to call him but I keep putting it off.

2 If you put a person off, you delay seeing them or doing what they want you to do.

She'll be here soon, unless I can put her off somehow.

show up

If you show up, you arrive at a place where people are expecting you.

I waited for half an hour, but she didn't show up.

NOTE   You can also use turn up.

stay in

If you stay in, you remain at home rather than going out.

We stayed in the whole evening.

NOTE   You can also use stop in.

NOTE   The opposite of stay in is go out.

take up

If you take up an activity or job, you start doing it.

I thought I'd take up fishing.

You're good at art. You should take it up professionally.

Exercise 1

Match verbs 1–4 with particles A–D to make phrasal verbs from this unit.

1 take / show / catch
2 eat / go / hang
3 stay / drop / get
4 come / go

A in
B out
C over
D up

Exercise 2

Complete the sentences with the phrasal verbs in the box.

drop in	hang out	showed up	come along	got together	call on

1 We could _____ your sister if we have time.
2 You could _____ to the cinema with us tonight, if you like.
3 Guang decided to _____ on his friend on the way to the park.
4 They _____ last week for lunch.
5 Lucas and Talia usually _____ at the shopping mall.
6 We waited for over an hour before Adam finally _____.

Exercise 3

Decide if the following sentences are true (*T*) or false (*F*).

1 When you eat out, you have a meal at a restaurant. ☐
2 The opposite of eat out is eat in. ☐
3 If you go out, you stay in your house. ☐
4 The opposite of go out is stay in. ☐
5 If you show up, you leave a place. ☐
6 If you hang out somewhere, you spend a lot of time there. ☐
7 If you take up an activity, you start doing it. ☐
8 If you call on someone, you move across a room. ☐

Exercise 4

Replace the underlined verbs with a phrasal verb from the box with the same meaning.

taken up	stay in	shows up	go over	went over	dropped in	drop in	come over

1 We were tired and decided just to stop in that night.
2 Why don't you come round about eight o'clock?
3 I popped in to see her on my way home.
4 What will we do if no one turns up?
5 I might go round to Mike's place later on.
6 Jen has started doing karate now.
7 After the game I went round to a friend's house.
8 If I have time I'll drop by and see her this afternoon.

Exercise 5

Match questions 1–6 with the correct replies A–F.

1 Why don't we call on Harry while we're in town?
2 What time should we call for you tomorrow?

3 We must catch up over dinner some time.

4 What time did you get in last night?
5 Can we meet with your parents this week?
6 I don't have any plans this evening.

A Oh, it was quite late … about midnight.
B How about this weekend? I know a great Italian restaurant.
C No, I think we should put off seeing them until next week.
D Good idea. Let's take him a present.
E Then why don't you come out to the party with me?
F Seven o'clock would be good.

Exercise 6

Complete the sentences with the correct form of the phrasal verbs in the box.

> put ... off | come along | ate out | catch up | get in | take up

1 I want to see the film but my husband keeps _____ it _____.
2 Why don't you _____ a new sport?
3 It's expensive to _____ to the night club, but the music is great.
4 I asked Brigitte to _____ with us to the show.
5 It was a good chance to _____ with some old friends.
6 When we lived in Los Angeles, we always _____ at the same restaurants.

Exercise 7

Correct the phrasal verbs in these sentences.

1 It was nice seeing you again. We must get up more often.
2 We're going to the cinema this evening. Would you like to come on with us?
3 What time shall I come off to your place tonight?
4 What time did you get over last night? Was it very late?
5 I don't feel like eating up tonight. I'll stay at home and cook something for dinner instead.
6 I've decided to take off yoga – they say it's a good form of exercise.

Exercise 8

Read the conversation. <u>Underline</u> all the phrasal verbs, then match them with the correct definitions 1–6.

> **Emma:** Hi Dylan. We're going to a concert tonight. Do you fancy coming along?
>
> **Dylan:** Sure! What time should we get together?
>
> **Emma:** Well, I was thinking we could go out around six thirty.
>
> **Dylan:** Okay, then I'll come over to your place at six.
>
> **Emma:** Great. Oh, I think we're going to eat out before the concert. And I'm taking my car. So how about we call for you at six instead?
>
> **Dylan:** Okay. See you then!

1 make a short visit _____
2 going with us to the same place _____
3 collect _____
4 leave the house _____
5 have a meal at a restaurant _____
6 meet _____

Your turn!

What do you enjoy doing in your leisure time? Use the phrasal verbs in this unit to talk about it. For example:

I like to get together with friends for dinner.

57

14

Sport and fitness

catch up

If you catch up or catch someone up, you reach someone who is in front of you by walking faster.

Simon tried to catch up with the others.

cut down

If you cut something down or cut down, you reduce the amount of something you use or eat, or do something less often.

We need to cut down the amount of fat in our diets.

You can cut the calories down a bit by adding less sugar.

fall behind

If you fall behind or fall behind someone when moving with a group of people, you move more slowly than them, so they get ahead of you.

Schumacher was strong throughout the race, but fell behind ten laps from the end.

NOTE   You can also use lag behind.

get into

1 If you get into a particular habit or way of behaving, you start to have that habit or behave in that way.

I really need to get into a fitness routine.

2 If you get into a subject, you start being interested in it. [INFORMAL]

She got into healthy eating and doing exercise.

go through

1 If someone goes through a series of actions or movements, they perform it.

The music started and we went through a series of warm-up exercises.

2 In sport, if a person or team goes through, they win one stage of a competition and go on to the next stage.

Serbia beat Russia 3–1 and look set to go through to round two.

go up

1 When someone or something goes up or goes up something, they move from a lower position to a higher one.

We saw a party of mountaineers going up the mountain.

NOTE   The opposite of go up is go down.

2 If a cheer, shout, or other noise goes up, a lot of people cheer, shout, or make that sound at the same time.

A huge cheer went up as the players walked out onto the court.

join in

If you join in or join in an activity, you start to do something with other people who are already doing it.

We joined in with the celebrations.

keep up

1 If you keep up an activity, you continue to do it and do not let it stop or end.

I can run fast over a short distance but I can't keep it up.

2 If you keep up, you move at the same speed as someone else.

Howard had to hurry to keep up with us.

slow down

1 If something or someone slows down, or if something or someone slows them down, they start to move or happen more slowly.

The driver slowed down and then stopped.

NOTE   The opposite of slow down is speed up.

2 If someone slows down, or if something slows them down, they become less active or energetic.

You're working too hard. You need to slow down.

He had an injured leg, which was slowing him down a little.

speed up

If something speeds up or if you speed it up, it moves or travels faster.

The driver sped up as he approached the lights.

wake up

When you wake up, or when someone or something wakes you up, you become conscious again after being asleep.

In the morning I wake up and feel refreshed.

wear out

If something wears you out, it makes you become so tired that you cannot continue what you were doing.

There is no point in wearing yourself out.

work on

If you work on something, you spend time and effort trying to improve it.

He has been working on his game all season.

NOTE   You can also use work at.

work out

If you work out, you do physical exercises in order to make your body healthy and strong.

She worked out in a gym class three hours a week.

work up

1 If someone works up a feeling, the energy to do something, or an appetite, they gradually develop it and increase it until they have what they need.

She went for a run to work up an appetite.

2 When you are doing something regularly, if you work up to a particular amount or level, you gradually increase or improve what you are doing until you reach that amount or level.

Repeat movements 1, 2 and 3 four times at first and gradually work up to about six repetitions.

NOTE   You can also use build up.

Exercise 1

Match the verbs with the particles to make phrasal verbs from this unit.

in | out | down | up

1 catch / keep / go / speed / wake / work / build   _____
2 cut / go / slow   _____
3 work / wear   _____
4 join   _____

Exercise 2

Match phrasal verbs 1–8 with the definitions A–H.

1 Tony's doctor told him to cut down his salt intake.
2 A long walk can help to work up a healthy appetite.
3 Cameroon and Egypt kick off the tournament this Saturday.
4 He fell so far behind that it was impossible to win the race.
5 The horse was tired and started to slow down.
6 He works out at the gym three times a week.
7 I got into yoga a few years ago.
8 Boxing has taught me that if you want something you've got to work hard at it.

A start being interested in something
B do physical exercises
C spend time and effort trying to improve something
D reduce something
E move more slowly so that other people get ahead of you
F start something
G gradually develop something
H start to move more slowly

Exercise 3

Complete the sentences. Choose the correct particles.

1 I'm putting on weight. I need to cut up / down / out on sugar and fats.
2 Our team has done really well – we've gone up / in / through to the finals.
3 I tried to get into / up / on yoga, but I found it boring.
4 If you aren't fit enough, you won't be able to keep out / up / through with the rest of the team.
5 He was coming last in the race, but he suddenly caught down / out / up and won!
6 My running shoes have worn up / in / out completely. I need some new ones.

Exercise 4

Complete the sentences with the words in the box.

keep | behind | went | up | into | go

1 The Spanish team now look certain to _____ through to the finals.
2 Your breathing will speed _____ after these exercises.
3 She'll need to run faster to _____ up with the other girls.
4 He was usually a fast runner, but he was starting to lag _____.
5 He _____ down the slope too quickly and fell over.
6 I got _____ the habit of drinking green tea every morning.

Exercise 5

Complete the newspaper headlines with the particles in the box.

DOWN | BEHIND | OFF | IN | THROUGH | UP

1 CROATIA GOES _____ TO THE FINALS!
2 FUEL PRICES GO _____ TO A RECORD HIGH THIS MONTH
3 HEALTH EXPERTS URGE PUBLIC TO CUT _____ THE AMOUNT OF SALT IN THEIR DIET
4 RECESSION CAUSES MORE AND MORE HOME OWNERS TO FALL _____ WITH MORTGAGE REPAYMENTS
5 MORE WORLD LEADERS JOIN _____ DEBATE ABOUT CLIMATE CHANGE
6 QUEEN'S BIRTHDAY CELEBRATIONS TO KICK _____ WITH GLOBAL POP CONCERT

Exercise 6

Make these sentences sound less formal. Replace the <u>underlined</u> verbs with the phrasal verbs in the box.

| joining in | sped up | slowed down | cut down | keep up | wear him out |

1 Daniel is trying to <u>reduce</u> his calorie intake.
2 The motorcycle <u>accelerated</u> shortly before it skidded off the track.
3 Running five times a week was starting to <u>exhaust him</u>.
4 I started cheering and soon everyone was <u>participating</u>.
5 It's important to <u>maintain</u> a balanced diet.
6 The car <u>decelerated</u> before coming to a stop.

Exercise 7

Read the extract from Bernard's fitness blog. <u>Underline</u> all the phrasal verbs, then in your own words, explain what each one means.

> I started getting into athletics when I was at school. As a professional athlete, my fitness level is something I have to work on all the time. In a typical training session I'll work up gradually so I don't wear myself out too quickly. When I wake up in the morning I like to do some yoga. Then I might work out at the gym for a couple of hours.

1 _____   4 _____
2 _____   5 _____
3 _____   6 _____

Exercise 8

Correct the phrasal verbs in these sentences.

1 It seemed impossible for him to catch in with the rest of the team.
2 Clark is confident the team can go off to the first division this year.
3 Michael scored just four minutes after they had kicked up.
4 She held the lead early in the race but now she's falling on.
5 You need to work over keeping fit.
6 Start slowly and build down to longer training sessions.
7 Unfortunately the team went over four goals to one.
8 Start getting onto the habit of walking to work.

Your turn!

Look for a website relating to a sport or fitness activity that interests you. Can you find any examples of the phrasal verbs in this unit?

He liked taking his dog for a walk every day, but didn't like to **wear** himself **out**.

Travel and tourism

check in

1. When you check in or when someone checks you in at a hotel, you arrive at the hotel, collect the key to your room, and fill in any forms which are necessary.

   I checked in at the Grand Hotel.

2. When you check in at an airport or when someone checks you in, you show your ticket before getting on the plane.

   He checked in without baggage for a flight to Rome.

   The remaining passengers were still being checked in.

check out

When you check out, you pay the bill at a hotel where you have been staying and leave.

She checked out of the hotel and took the train to Paris.

come across

If you come across someone or something, you find or meet them by chance.

As they walked round the lake they came across a bridge.

come from

If you come from a particular place, you were born there or grew up there.

Nuria comes from Madrid.

drop off

When you are driving, if you drop off a person or thing, you take them somewhere and leave them there, usually on your way to somewhere else.

I can drop her off on my way home.

I need to drop off some books at the office.

get away

1. If you get away, you succeed in leaving a place or person.

   If I'm lucky I might get away by midnight.

2. If you get away, you go somewhere to have a holiday.

   Is there any chance of you getting away this summer?

get back

If you get back, you return somewhere after being in another place.

We didn't get back till midnight last night.

get in

1. If you get in or get in a place such as a car, house, or room, you go inside it.

   She got in and started the car.

   I got in a taxi and went to the airport.

   NOTE   The opposite of get in is get out.

2. When a person or a vehicle gets in, they arrive at a place where people are expecting them to be.

   Her train should get in at 6:30 p.m.

get into

1 If you get into a place such as a car, house, or room, you enter it.

They got into the back of a taxi.

2 If a person or vehicle gets into a place, they reach it.

We got into London at one o'clock.

get off

1 If you get off or get off a bus, train, or plane, you leave a bus, train, or plane.

I slipped as I was getting off the train.

NOTE   You can also use get out.

NOTE   The opposite of get off is get on.

2 When you get off, you leave somewhere, often to start a journey.

I plan to get off before the traffic gets bad.

NOTE   You can also use get away.

go around

1 If you go around or go around a group of people or places, you visit or go to see people or places, one after the other.

I want to go around the art galleries while I'm in London.

NOTE   You can also use go round. This is mainly British.

2 If you go around or go around a country or other place, you travel in a country or other place and visit a lot of different things.

I'd like to go around Africa myself.

NOTE   You can also use go round. This is mainly British.

go away

1 If you go away, you leave somewhere.

She went away to think about it.

2 If you go away, you leave your home and spend time somewhere else, especially as a holiday.

What did you do over the summer? Did you go away?

head for

If you head for a place, you start moving towards it.

We had decided to head for Miami.

NOTE   You can also use make for.

move on

If someone moves on, they continue a journey after stopping for a short time.

After three weeks in Hong Kong, we moved on to Japan.

NOTE   You can also use carry on.

set off

When you set off, you start a journey.

What time do we need to set off tomorrow?

NOTE   You can also use set out.

Exercise 1

Complete the sentences. Choose the correct particles.

1 We checked *at / to / in* early for our flight.
2 We came *across / back / away* a beautiful castle in the mountains.
3 Our plane got *on / away / into* Beijing two hours late.
4 Yuriko and Daisuke are going *round / out / up* Europe next year.
5 They set *at / over /off* at six o'clock this morning.
6 We all got *into / over /away* the car and drove to the beach.
7 The ship set *at / out /on* for Australia via Africa.
8 We stay in Bali for two days, then we move *at / with /on* to Brisbane.

Exercise 2

Match phrasal verbs 1–8 with definitions A–H.

1 check in
2 check out
3 drop off
4 get back
5 get off
6 head for
7 come from
8 go away

A take something somewhere and leave it there
B leave a bus, train, or plane
C leave a place
D pay the bill and leave a hotel
E start moving towards
F arrive at a hotel
G return from somewhere
H be born or grow up somewhere

Exercise 3

Decide if the following sentences are true (*T*) or false (*F*).

1 If you come across something, you find it by chance. ☐
2 If you head for a place, you avoid it. ☐
3 If you set off, you start a journey. ☐
4 If you drop something off, you can't find it. ☐
5 If you move on, you leave your home to live in a new one. ☐
6 If you get away for a few days, you have a holiday. ☐

Exercise 4

Replace the <u>underlined</u> verbs with a phrasal verb from the box with the same meaning.

| moved on | headed for | went around | get off | got off | came across |

1 Did Gina <u>get away</u> okay this morning?
2 They watched as the driver <u>got out</u> the train.
3 It started to rain, so she <u>made for</u> the hotel.
4 We waited for the rain to stop before we <u>carried on</u> to the next town.
5 We <u>found</u> a lovely seafood restaurant.
6 We <u>went round</u> some of the museums in Florence.

Exercise 5

Complete the holiday adverts with the particles in the box.

| IN | FOR | AWAY | AWAY | AROUND | ACROSS |

1 GET _____ TO THAILAND THIS SUMMER FOR JUST $500!
2 HEAD _____ THE SUN! 50 PER CENT OFF FLIGHTS TO SPAIN.
3 CHECK _____ TO OUR HOTEL THIS WEEKEND AND GET THREE NIGHTS FOR THE PRICE OF TWO!
4 YOU WON´T COME _____ THE SAME HOLIDAY CHEAPER ELSEWHERE!
5 BUY INSURANCE BEFORE YOU GO _____.
6 GO _____ THE WORLD IN JUST ONE MONTH!

Exercise 6

Correct the phrasal verbs in these sentences.

1 He's going to go in Europe with a friend for three months.
2 Welcome home! When did you get away from holiday?
3 It's a lovely, sunny day. Let's head off the beach today.
4 You have to get up the bus at the last stop.
5 You can check out online, to save yourself time at the airport.
6 What time does your train get on at the station?

Exercise 7

Complete the sentences with the correct form of the phrasal verbs in the box.

come from	get in	get away	get off	drop … off	check out	get into	check in

1 If I can _____ early from work I'll be home quicker.
2 All guests must _____ of the hotel before 12 p.m.
3 'Where do you _____?'—'I'm from Bangladesh.'
4 We need to _____ at the next stop.
5 What time does your train _____ Berlin?
6 Our coach _____ at eight o'clock last night.
7 When you arrive, please _____ at the reception desk.
8 The coach can _____ passengers _____ at various hotels on the island.

Exercise 8

Read the hotel review. <u>Underline</u> all the phrasal verbs, then answer the questions.

> **THE GEORGE HOTEL ****
>
> Our plane got into London very late – at about 2 a.m. But the staff were friendly and helpful when we checked in. The hotel is ideally located for going around the main tourist attractions in the city centre. We came across an excellent Indian restaurant next door, which I'd recommend. We're planning on getting away for a short holiday next year. I think we will definitely head for the George Hotel!

1 When did the plane arrive in London?
2 How were the staff when they arrived?
3 What is the hotel in a good location for?
4 What did they find next to the hotel?
5 What are they planning next year?
6 Where will they stay?

Your turn!

Think about a holiday you enjoyed or a place you have travelled to. Use the phrasal verbs in this unit to talk about your experience. For example:

We set off on our trip very early in the morning.

I think we **got off** at the wrong stop.

16

Clothing and fashion

do up

1 If you do something up, you fasten it.

She showed her son how to do up his shoes.

I can't do my top button up.

2 If a piece of clothing does up in a particular place, it is fastened there.

The top does up at the back.

3 If a woman does her hair up, she arranges it so that it is fastened close to her head rather than hanging loosely.

She did her hair up in a pony tail.

Her hair was done up in a neat bun at the back of her head.

dress up

1 If you dress up or dress someone up, you put special, smart clothes on yourself or someone else, usually for a social occasion.

It's fun to dress up for a party.

I like to dress my little girl up in pretty clothes.

2 If you dress up or dress someone up, you put special costumes or unusual clothes on yourself or someone else, usually for fun, often at a party where everyone does this.

Maisie loves to dress up in her Grandma's clothes.

We dressed Alex up as Superman for Amelia's party.

get on

If you get a piece of clothing on, you dress yourself in it.

Get your coat on.

NOTE   You can also use put on.

go with

If one thing goes with another, they suit each other or are pleasant or attractive together.

Those shoes go with your dress.

have on

If you have clothing on, you are wearing it.

I can't wait to take these shoes off – I've had them on all day.

She had on an old jacket.

pick out

If you pick out one thing, you choose it from a group.

Christina picked out a nice pair of shoes to wear.

She picked a skirt out that she thought Ellie would like.

pull off

When you pull a piece of clothing off or pull a piece of clothing off someone else, you take it off quickly.

I managed to pull my boots off.

James pulled off his socks.

I pulled Tom's boots off his feet.

pull on

When you pull on your clothes, you put them on quickly.

Still sitting, he pulled his shirt and trousers on.

put on

1 When you put on a piece of clothing, you put it over a part of your body and wear it, or you put it over a part of someone else's body so they are wearing it.

She put her coat on.

NOTE   The opposite of put on is take off.

2 When you put on make-up, a cream, or perfume, you spread or spray it on your skin.

Make sure you put some suncream on before you go out.

show off

If you show off something that you own, you show it to a lot of people because you are proud of it.

They held out their arms, showing off their jewellery.

He bought her a ring and she has been showing it off to everyone.

take in

If you take something in, you make an item of clothing smaller and tighter.

He lost so much weight that he had to take in all his trousers.

NOTE   The opposite of take in is let out.

take up

If you take up a piece of clothing, you make it shorter.

I can take up those trousers for you.

NOTE   The opposite of take up is let down.

try on

If you try on a piece of clothing, you put it on to see if it fits you or if it looks nice.

She tried on several dresses but couldn't find any she liked.

wear out

When something wears out or when you wear it out, it is used so much that it becomes weak or broken and unable to be used any more.

Sooner or later the soles of your favourite shoes are going to wear out.

He did not want them walking up and down the stairs and wearing out the stair carpet.

wrap up

1 When you wrap something up, you fold a piece of paper, cloth, or other material round it so that it is completely covered.

We wrapped the glasses up in tissue paper.

My hair is wrapped up in a towel because I've just washed it.

NOTE   You can also use do up.

2 If you wrap up, you put warm clothes on; if you wrap someone, especially a child, up, you put warm clothes on them.

Wrap up well. It's cold outside.

The children came to school wrapped up in coats and scarves.

Exercise 1

Match the particles with the verbs to make phrasal verbs from this unit.

off | on | out | up

1 do / dress / take / wrap _____
2 try / put / have / get _____
3 wear / pick _____
4 pull / show _____

Exercise 2

Complete the sentences with the particles in the box.

up | on | out | off | with | in

1 The dresses were all so pretty, it was hard to pick _____ the nicest one.
2 He untied his shoes and took them _____.
3 She always likes to dress _____ when we go out to dinner.
4 That T-shirt doesn't really go _____ those shoes.
5 These trousers are too wide – I'll need to take them _____.
6 Try this dress _____ and see if it fits.

Exercise 3

Match phrasal verbs 1–6 with definitions A–F.

1 When it's cold outside you need to wrap up warm!
2 The shorts are one size too big, but you can take them in.
3 It was hot so Cameron pulled off his sweater.
4 Her dress was too long, so she decided to take it up a little.
5 He did up the buttons of his shirt.
6 Children can wear their shoes out quickly.

A fasten something
B take something off quickly
C use something so much it becomes weak
D make clothing smaller or tighter
E make clothing shorter
F put warm clothes on

Exercise 4

Decide if the following sentences are true (*T*) or false (*F*).

1 Take off means the opposite of put on. ☐
2 Take in means the opposite of let out. ☐
3 Take up means the same as let down. ☐
4 Get on means the same as put on. ☐
5 Show off means the same as take in. ☐
6 Have on means the same as pull on. ☐

Exercise 5

Match sentence halves 1–8 with A–H to make complete sentences.

1 I've worn this jumper so often
2 I tried on a gorgeous scarf,
3 She pulled on her socks
4 It was difficult to pull my
5 Can you pick out something nice
6 He had on
7 Does this handbag go
8 Alicia did her hair

A and went out the door.
B for me to wear tonight?
C blue jeans and a grey T-shirt.
D I think I've worn it out!
E with my new shoes?
F up for the wedding.
G but it was too expensive, so I didn't buy it.
H ski boots off.

Exercise 6

Match phrasal verbs 1–6 with a word or phrase with the same meaning A–F.

1 I don't think that dress goes with that jacket.   **A** arrange
2 These trousers are too long. I need to take them up.   **B** chose
3 She picked out a beautiful dress for the wedding.   **C** matches
4 Everyone was talking about what the celebrities had   **D** shorten
   on at the premiere.
5 Is it a casual party, or do we need to dress up?   **E** wore
6 It took me ages to do up my hair in this style.   **F** wear formal clothes

Exercise 7

Complete the sentences with the phrasal verbs in the box.

| took ... off | show off | put on | got ... on | dress up | did up |

1 When Jayden was younger, he liked to _____ in a super hero costume.
2 He grabbed his jacket, _____ it _____ and walked out the door.
3 Why don't you _____ your new aftershave?
4 The event gave the actress a chance to _____ her new hairstyle.
5 She wore an unusual dress that _____ at the front.
6 He _____ his hat _____ and sat down in the shade.

Exercise 8

Read the conversation. <u>Underline</u> all the phrasal verbs, then decide if the sentences that follow are true (*T*) or false (*F*).

Isabella: Hi. I'd like to try on this dress, please. I'm not sure about the size, though …

Store Assistant: No problem. You can put it on in the changing room over there. If the dress doesn't fit we can take it in for you.

Isabella: Thanks. Could you pick out some shoes to match the dress?

Store Assistant: Of course. How about these silver shoes? They go really well with it.

Isabella: Oh yes, they're much nicer than the shoes I have on!

1 Isabella asks if she can put on the dress to see if it fits her. ☐
2 The assistant tells her it will not be possible to wear the dress. ☐
3 The assistant offers to make the dress smaller, if needed. ☐
4 Isabella asks the assistant to choose a handbag for her. ☐
5 The assistant thinks the shoes look attractive with the dress. ☐
6 Isabella prefers the silver shoes to the ones she is wearing. ☐

Your turn!

Think about clothes or fashions that you like. Use the phrasal verbs in this unit to talk about them. For example:

When I'm cold I like to put on my favourite sweater.

I enjoy dressing up in the latest styles.

They realised that they both **had on** the same dress.

Studying and learning

catch up

If a person or thing catches up or catches someone or something up, they reach the same standard or level.

Once you become so behind with your studies, it's really hard to catch up.

They did well early on, but other businesses are catching them up now.

cut out

If you cut out part of something, you remove it by cutting it.

She had cut out pictures of animals and stuck them on the wall.

I cut an article out of the paper and sent it to her.

drop out

If you drop out, you leave something that you are involved in before it is finished.

She had dropped out of college in the first term.

He dropped out of school and went to work in the supermarket.

fall behind

If someone or something falls behind or falls behind someone or something, they do not reach the standard or level of similar people or things.

These children often fall behind with their reading.

His salary has fallen behind those of many of his colleagues.

find out

If you find out something, you learn something that you did not already know.

I'm only interested in finding out what the facts are.

I used the Internet to find their names out.

go over

If you go over something, you examine or discuss each part of it, especially to make sure that someone understands it or that it is correct.

I'll go over the main points of what she said.

hand in

If you hand in a piece of work, you give it to someone so that they can read it or deal with it.

At half-past eleven they handed their exam papers in.

Don't forget to hand in your homework.

hand out

If you hand things out, you give them to people in a group so that each person has one or some.

They handed out questionnaires to the audience.

The teacher asked me to hand the books out.

look at

☐1 If you look at something or someone, you turn your eyes towards them.

Everyone turned to look at the painting.

☐2 If you look at something, you quickly read it or read parts of it.

I've looked at your essay and I think it's very good.

NOTE   You can also use look through.

☐3 If you look at a subject, problem, or situation, you consider or study it.

His research looked at the way language is acquired.

look up

☐1 If you look up, you raise your eyes.

She did not even look up from her work when he came in

☐2 If you look something up, you find a piece of information by looking at something such as a book or website.

He used a dictionary to look up the word 'apotheosis'.

Nowadays you can look almost anything up on the Internet.

miss out

If you miss out something or someone, you fail to include them in something. [BRITISH]

The brochure had missed out the fact that the hotel was right by a busy road.

He missed some important details out of his report.

NOTE   You can also use leave out. [mainly AMERICAN]

mix up

If you mix things or people up, you are confused about which one is which.

I think you're mixing up the American Civil War with the English Civil War.

Do you have a tendency to mix the digits up when trying to remember numbers?

opt for

If you opt for a particular thing, you decide to do or have that thing.

Unsure what to study at university, she eventually opted for Law.

relate to

If something relates to a particular subject, it is about that subject or is connected with it.

I wanted to ask you a question that relates to electricity.

run through

If you run through something, you explain it or read it quickly, in order to practise it, check it or make sure that people understand it.

Some of you won't know this so I'll just briefly run through it.

NOTE   You can also use go through and run over.

sign up

If you sign up, you sign an agreement to do a job or course of study, or join an organization.

She signed up to do a Masters degree after graduating from Columbia.

take in

If you take something in, you pay attention to it so that you understand, remember, or experience it fully.

I didn't take in everything that he was saying.

Alex had been the perfect pupil, listening and watching and taking it in.

Exercise 1

Match the verbs with the particles to make phrasal verbs from this unit.

through | up | behind | to | out | for

1 catch / look / mix / sign   _____
2 cut / drop / find / hand /leave / miss _____
3 run / look / go   _____
4 opt   _____
5 relate   _____
6 fall   _____

Exercise 2

Match phrasal verbs 1–8 with definitions A–H.

1 Andrew found the course difficult and dropped out after a month.
2 They were discussing a complex idea, so it was hard to take it all in.
3 Dana missed two classes, so it took her a while to catch up.
4 At university Elias opted for political history and economics.
5 This chapter relates closely to the last one.
6 I looked up his address on the company website.
7 She handed out the certificates to everyone in the class.
8 He went over the instructions with me again to make sure I understood.

A find information in a book or website
B leave something you are involved in before it is finished
C decide to do something
D be connected with something
E pay attention so that you understand something
F give things out to people in a group
G discuss something to make sure someone understands it
H reach the same standard or level as someone else

Exercise 3

Complete the sentences. Choose the best answers.

1 If you don't know the meaning of a word, look it *up / through / over*.
2 I want to find *over / out / up* more information about this subject.
3 Would you mind running *at / behind / through* the details once more, just so I am quite clear?
4 You've missed *up / in / out* a full stop at the end of that sentence.
5 Many students drop *out / in / up* of university during the first year.
6 There's too much information here to take *up / over / in* at once.

Exercise 4

Answer the questions.

1 If you opt for something, do you choose to do it or not?
2 If you hand something out, do you give it to someone or take it from someone?
3 If you sign up for something, do you agree or disagree to become involved with it?
4 If you need to catch up on work, are you at the same standard as others, or below it?
5 If you go over some work, do you repeat it or examine it closely?
6 If you run through some work, do you do it quickly or in detail?

Exercise 5

Complete the sentences with the phrasal verbs in the box.

looks at | cut out | run through | handed in | fall behind | missed ... out

1 She _____ pictures from magazines for her art project.
2 If you miss too many classes, you might _____ in your studies.
3 He _____ the essay to his teacher a day late.
4 The film _____ the fascinating history of the country.
5 I think you have _____ a few things _____ in your report.
6 I'll just _____ a quick summary of the findings.

Exercise 6

Replace the <u>underlined</u> verbs with a phrasal verb from the box with the same meaning.

> finding out | looks at | run through | looking through
> take in | went over | missed ... out | mix up

1 I was <u>looking at</u> your report when I noticed a mistake.
2 The name is spelled with an 'e' at the end – you've <u>left</u> it <u>out</u>.
3 First, let me <u>go through</u> today's agenda.
4 Try not to <u>confuse</u> the two issues.
5 In her book she <u>considers</u> the position of women in society.
6 I was able to <u>understand</u> most of what he was saying.
7 I enjoy <u>learning</u> about different cultures in the world.
8 We <u>discussed</u> the results in great detail.

Exercise 7

Read Ruby's comments about her university degree. <u>Underline</u> all the phrasal verbs, then match them with the correct definitions 1–6.

> After I finished high school, I signed up to do a degree in Biology at Leeds University. I wanted to find out more about Biotechnology, so I opted for a short course on it during my first semester. At first it was a lot to take in and I was worried I would fall behind. But my tutor went over the coursework with me and by the end of the year I passed the course.

1 not reach the same standard or level as other people
2 signed an agreement to do a course of study
3 understand something
4 learn something
5 helped me to understand something by talking about it
6 decided to do something

Exercise 8

Complete the sentences with the correct form of the phrasal verbs in the box.

> drop out | relate to | run over | hand in | find out | sign up

1 Professor Jeong _____ to the organization last May.
2 We'll begin by _____ the recommended reading material for this course.
3 These figures do not _____ patients over the age of 65.
4 If you want to _____ more, click on the link below.
5 Jason _____ of school at the age of 14.
6 Please _____ your reports to your teacher by next Wednesday.

Your turn!

What would you like to learn more about? Use the phrasal verbs in this unit to talk about this. For example:

I'd like to find out more about the history of my country.

I'll just run through my speech one more time.

18

Jobs and careers

carry out

If you carry out a task, you do it.

They have to carry out a number of administrative duties.

The team carried a survey out and its findings were interesting.

fit in

If you fit in, you are happy and accepted in a group of people because you are similar to the other people in it.

You have to learn how the company works in order to fit in.

We're looking for someone who will fit in with our team.

get out of

1. If you get something good, especially pleasure or satisfaction, out of something that you do or experience, you enjoy it or find it useful.

I get a lot of satisfaction out of my job.

2. If you get out of doing something, you avoid doing it.

If there was work to be done around the house, Alec would always get out of it.

He'll do anything to get out of going to visit his grandparents.

NOTE   You can also use wriggle out of.

lay off

If workers are laid off or if their employer lays them off, they are told that they have to leave their jobs for a period of time or permanently, because there is no work for them to do.

City workers are being laid off at the rate of 100 a week.

Her employer laid her off eight months later.

Factories are warning that they may have to lay off workers.

make up

If people or things make up something, they form it. If something is made up of people or things, they form it.

Women now make up two-fifths of the work force.

The EU's budget has to be agreed by the member states that make it up.

Nearly half the Congress is made up of lawyers.

move into

If people move into a particular activity or area of business, they start to be involved in it.

She later moved into the field of education.

move out of

If people move out of a particular activity or area of business, research, etc., they stop being involved in it.

People are moving out of the public sector and into the private sector.

set up

If you set something up, you make the necessary arrangements for it to start.

The software billionaire set up a development agency to work in Africa.

She set a meeting up for me with the Managing Director.

settle in

If you settle in or you are settled in, you become used to a new place or new job.

How is he settling in to his new job?

My colleagues were very helpful while I was getting settled in.

shut down

1 If someone shuts down a factory or business or if it shuts down, it closes and stops working.

They shut down the water plants and told residents to buy bottled water.

The company would be forced to shut the whole factory down.

More than 50 businesses in the town have shut down this year.

NOTE You can also use close down.

2 If a machine or an engine shuts down or if it is shut down, it stops working for a short time.

His computer overheated and shut down.

There was supposed to be an emergency mechanism for shutting down the system.

The reactor's automatic controls shut it down.

NOTE You can also use shut off.

stay on

If you stay on, you remain in a place or continue to attend it regularly. [BRITISH]

After his contract finished, he agreed to stay on for another three months.

step down

If you step down, you leave an important job or position.

The CEO stepped down last month because of illness.

NOTE You can also use step aside and stand down.

stick out

1 If something or someone sticks out, they are very obvious or noticeable, especially because of being very different from things or people around them.

He wore a dark grey suit that would not stick out in any workplace.

NOTE You can also use stand out.

2 If you stick something out, you continue in a difficult or unpleasant situation, rather than leaving it.

Sometimes I wonder if I can stick this job out much longer.

take off

If you take time off, you spend it doing something different from your normal activities or job.

I won't be here tomorrow as I'm taking the day off.

Your contract entitles you to take off twenty days a year.

take on

1 If you take on a job, task, or responsibility, you accept it and try to do what is required.

She takes on more work than is good for her.

It's a big responsibility and it's nice of him to take it on.

2 If someone takes you on, they employ you.

They took me on because I was a good mathematician.

In the current climate, employers are taking on less people.

walk out

If workers walk out, they suddenly stop working and leave the place where they work as a protest.

Up to 60,000 staff will walk out next month in support of a 40 per cent pay rise.

Exercise 1

Decide if the following sentences are true (*T*) or false (*F*).

1 If workers are laid off, they are told they must leave their jobs. ☐
2 If you take time off, you remain in your place of work. ☐
3 If you step down, you leave an important job. ☐
4 If someone takes you on, they tell you to leave your job. ☐
5 If you fit in, you are happy and accepted by a group of people. ☐
6 If you settle in, you become used to a new job. ☐

Exercise 2

Match sentence halves 1–6 with A–F to make complete sentences.

1 Cathy decided to stay on at the company
2 I'm really keen to set up
3 It's a very friendly office and I
4 The head office has decided
5 We all think the manager
6 I can't take off another day –

A my own business one day.
B after her work experience ended.
C I've just had two weeks holiday this year.
D should step down after the scandal about his expenses claims.
E found it easy to settle in.
F to shut down three branches of the business.

Exercise 3

Complete the sentences with the phrasal verbs in the box.

| shut ... down | got ... out of | walked out | made up of | stick ... out | stay on | moving into | step down |

1 He wasn't sure whether to _____ at school or leave and get a job.
2 Zack hated his job, but he decided to _____ it _____ until he found something better.
3 Angelique was thinking of leaving the accounts team and _____ marketing.
4 The seminar was extremely dull – I _____ very little _____it.
5 The business isn't doing well. In fact, we may have to _____ it _____.
6 Our team is _____ five men and five women.
7 Peter offered to _____ from his position.
8 Hundreds of workers _____ in the dispute.

Exercise 4

Replace the underlined verbs with a phrasal verb from the box with the same meaning.

| get out of | shut down | shut down | step down | stick out | make up | carry out | set up |

1 We arranged a meeting between both departments for the next day.
2 Most of the work I do is of a technical nature.
3 I don't want to give this presentation, but I can't wriggle out of it.
4 I'm sorry to say that our production manager has decided to stand down.
5 International orders form over 50 per cent of our business.
6 Please remember to shut off your computer before you leave.
7 I like to wear bright colours to work so that I stand out.
8 Unfortunately we had to close down three of our stores last year.

Exercise 5

Complete the job adverts with the particles in the box.

| OUT | IN | UP | ON | OUT OF | INTO |

1 SET _____ YOUR OWN BUSINESS!
2 CAN YOU FIT _____ WITH OUR WAY OF THINKING?
3 TAKE _____ A BIGGER CHALLENGE!
4 MOVE _____ WEB-BASED MEDIA
5 GET MORE _____ YOUR CAREER
6 HELP US BY CARRYING _____ WORK SURVEYS

Exercise 6

Correct the phrasal verbs in these sentences.

1 Do you have everything you need in order to carry off the task?
2 We regret to announce that we have to lay down some members of staff.
3 We're taking in three new employees this month.
4 She's not happy in her work, but she's decided to stick it up until she finds something else.
5 She used to work in the public sector but she's moved up the private sector now.
6 Are you the kind of person who will be able to fit on with our way of doing things?

Exercise 7

Match questions 1–6 with the correct replies A–F.

1 How is your new job going?
2 Why did they have to lay off so many workers?
3 What made you decide to move out of teaching?
4 Do you mind staying on after work to help me with this?
5 Why don't you take some time off?
6 Do you think that you fit in at your work?

A Because the business was doing really badly.
B Good idea. I really need a rest.
C I wanted to try something new.
D It's going great. I'm really settling in now.
E No, not at all. I'm happy to help if I can.
F Yes I do – I get on well with all my colleagues.

Exercise 8

Read the job advert. <u>Underline</u> all the phrasal verbs, then in your own words, explain what each one means.

> **WANTED: WEB DESIGNER**
> Do you think you can fit in with a small, dynamic team? Does your CV stand out from the rest? Then we want to take you on! We have recently set up a small media company and need someone to design a new web-based application. Your duties will include carrying out regular tests and you must be willing to take on new challenges. Click below to apply now!

1 _____ 4 _____
2 _____ 5 _____
3 _____ 6 _____

Your turn!

Think about the job you do now, or a job you would like to do. Use the phrasal verbs in this unit to talk about it. For example:

It took me a long time to settle in.

I'd like to take on a more challenging role.

19

Business

bring out

When a person or company brings out a new product, they produce it and sell it.

The company is planning to bring out a new range of financial products later this year.

The singer has now brought a second album out.

build on

1 If an activity, organization, system or belief is built on something, it is developed from that thing.

The relationship between a bank and its customer is built on trust.

NOTE   You can also use build upon and base on.

2 If you build on the success of something, you take advantage of it to make further progress.

We must try to build on the success of these industries.

They are building on existing skills and traditions.

come out of

If one thing comes out of something else, the first thing results from the second.

If all you focus on is negative thinking, then nothing good can come out of it.

hand over

1 If you hand something over, you give it to someone so that they have or own it.

He handed the phone over to me.

People have handed over large sums of money for work that was never done.

2 If you hand over to someone or hand something over, you give another person responsibility for dealing with something.

The head teacher handed over to his deputy.

He recently handed control of the company over to his son.

keep down

If someone or something keeps the number, size, or amount of something down, they stop it increasing and keep it at a low level.

They employ fewer staff to keep costs down.

We need to keep down production costs.

look into

If you look into something, you find out and examine the facts about a problem or situation.

They hired a financial adviser to look into the firm's accounts.

make up for

To make up for something means to replace something that has been lost or damaged or to provide something instead of it.

There would have to be major cuts to make up for the loss of revenue.

pull out

1 If you pull out, you decide not to continue with an activity or agreement.

They pulled out of the deal at the last minute.

NOTE   You can also use back out.

2 If you pull someone out, you decide not to continue with an activity or agreement.

The singer's new manager pulled her out of the book deal.

send off

If you send something off, you send it somewhere by post, email, or text message.

I sent off letters of enquiry to all the big firms.

It's a good idea to re-read your emails before you send them off.

send out

If you send something out, you send copies of something to a lot of people.

The company sent out questionnaires to 34,000 doctors.

We send regular newsletters out to our customers.

start up

If you start something up, or if you start up, you start a new business or project; if a business starts up, it begins.

She wanted to start up her own business.

There are a lot of additional costs when you are starting up.

NOTE   You can also use set up.

take off

If something takes off, it becomes very successful or popular.

If the product takes off, you could make your money back within a year.

take over

To take over a business means to gain control of it by buying it or buying a majority of its shares.

The I.P.C. was taken over by the Reed Paper Group.

He's made a great success of the restaurant since he took it over.

NOTE   You can also use buy out.

team up

If two or more people or organizations team up, they join together in order to do something.

That year, NBC teamed up with Microsoft to launch the news channel MSNBC.

try out

If you try out something or try something out, you test it or use it for the first time in order to find out how useful or effective it is.

The company is trying out a new idea to help working parents.

First they tried it out on a small group of people.

turn around

If something such as a plan, project, or business that is failing turns around or if you turn it around, it starts to become successful or profitable.

The project is not going well, but I'm confident I can turn it around.

He believes he can turn around last year's losses and make a profit.

NOTE   You can also use turn round. This is mainly British.

Exercise 1

Match the verbs with the particles to make phrasal verbs from this unit.

out | off | up | over | on | down

1 base / build _____   4 set / start / team _____
2 back / bring / buy / pull / send / try _____   5 keep _____
3 send / take _____   6 hand / take _____

Exercise 2

Complete the sentences. Choose the correct particles.

1 The manager would like us to team *together* / *out* / *up* to do the next task.
2 The sales in Korea will make *down* / *up* / *out* for the loss of sales in Europe.
3 His first business idea really took *off* / *away* / *up* and he now runs a very successful company.
4 I wish they'd would bring *around* / *off* / *out* a product that could charge all electronic devices with one single charger!
5 Remember to send the package *over* / *up* / *off* by airmail, in order to get it there on time.
6 We're downsizing in order to keep costs *out* / *down* / *off*.

Exercise 3

Match phrasal verbs 1–8 with definitions A–H.

1 This is a bad situation. Nothing good can come out of it.   A find out the facts about something
2 The manager said she would look into the matter and then contact us.   B produce and sell something
3 The extra sales we made this month will make up for our losses last month.   C provide something as a replacement
4 The new director has really turned the company around.   D result from something
5 Next year the company plans to bring out a new version of the phone.   E start a new business or project
6 We want to build on our strong brand identity.   F make something become successful or profitable
7 We didn't have much money when we first started up.   G stop something increasing and keep at a low level
8 Costs should be kept down at a reasonable level.   H take advantage of something to make progress

Exercise 4

Complete the news headlines with the particles in the box.

UP | UP | OVER | OVER | OFF | AROUND

1 D&Z SET TO TAKE _____ SMALLER COMPANY
2 GERBER TO TEAM _____ WITH HUANG
3 NEW PRODUCT LINE TAKES _____
4 DANIELS TO HAND _____ CONTROL OF BUSINESS
5 MORE BUSINESSES TO START _____ IN NORTH EAST
6 CONSULTANT TURNS COMPANY _____

Exercise 5

Replace the underlined verbs with a phrasal verb from the box with the same meaning.

turn ... around | taken over | starting up | pull out | look into | built on

1 Our business is built upon creative thinking.
2 Kostwize has said it might back out of negotiations with Zentron.
3 Beverley has always dreamed of setting up her own production company.
4 The firm could be bought out as early as next month.
5 We'll need to turn things round if we want to survive in this market.
6 Management will investigate the causes of these incidents.

Exercise 6

Make these sentences sound less formal. Replace the <u>underlined</u> verbs with the phrasal verbs in the box.

| trying out | to pull out of | take over | turn around | look into it | send out |

1 If anyone can <u>make a success of</u> a business, it will be him.
2 How often do you <u>post</u> promotional material?
3 The company decided <u>not to go ahead with</u> investing in Europe.
4 I don't know the answer just yet, but I'll <u>do some research and find out</u>.
5 She's a bossy person, who always tries to <u>control</u> meetings.
6 We're <u>testing</u> a new service on some volunteers at the moment.

Exercise 7

Read Jonathan's comments about his business. <u>Underline</u> all the phrasal verbs, then answer the questions.

> I started up my own business three years ago. At first things really took off – I was making lots of money and the customers were happy with my products. I tried hard to build on my good relationship with customers. But the economy is weak now, so people are less willing to hand over money. We'll need to keep our costs down for the business to survive another year. I really hope the economy turns around soon.

1 When did Jonathan start his business?
2 Was it successful in the first year?
3 What did Jonathan try to take advantage of?
4 Why don't people want to spend money now?
5 What must he keep at a low level?
6 What does he hope will improve?

Exercise 8

Complete the sentences with the correct form of the phrasal verbs in the box.

| team up | come out of | make up for | hand over | send out | try out |

1 We lost a lot of money, but hopefully we'll _____ it next year.
2 She asked her assistant to _____ the email to everyone in the company.
3 The company is _____ the new product on a small test group at the moment.
4 It was a difficult year, but I have _____ it a better and stronger person.
5 Never _____ money in advance to a trader you know nothing about.
6 The company has _____ with a Korean electronics firm to produce the MP3 players.

Your turn!

Look at websites relating to business. Can you find any examples of the phrasal verbs in this unit?

He never enjoyed **handing over** money.

Money and spending

amount to

If something amounts to a particular sum or number, its total is that quantity.

She lost all her savings, which amounted to a large sum of money.

NOTE   You can also use add up to.

bring in

Someone or something that brings in money, or brings money in, makes or earns it.

Tourism is a big industry, bringing in £7 billion a year.

We will have to consider how we can bring funds in.

build up

If something builds up or if you build it up, it gradually increases in amount, size, or strength.

Money built up in your savings can be used to boost your retirement income.

We helped to build up the wealth of this country.

The city must build its cash reserves up to a more comfortable level.

come into

If someone comes into money, property, or a title, they get it when someone in their family dies.

She came into some money on her mother's death.

cut back on

If you cut back on the money that you spend on something, you reduce it.

The government has had to cut back on public spending.

get into

If you get into a difficult situation, or if someone gets you into it, you start to be involved in it, often without intending to be.

Make sure you don't get into debt.

He got himself into such a mess.

give away

If you give away something, or give something away, you give it to someone without taking money in return.

She has given away jewellery worth millions of dollars.

I couldn't decide whether to keep the money he left me or give it away.

live on

If you live on an amount of money, you have that amount of money to buy things.

I don't have enough to live on.

pay for

1 If you pay for something, you give someone money for it.

We have to have money to pay for the food we eat.

2 If something that you buy pays for itself, it saves you as much money as you spent on it.

These water heaters are more efficient and will pay for themselves within five years.

pay in

When you pay in money, or pay money in, you put it into a bank account.

Roberto called in at the bank to pay his cheque in.

I paid in £150 this morning.

pay off

If you pay off a debt or bill, you pay all the money that you owe.

The most common reason for borrowing is to pay off existing loans.

She paid her debts off by selling her house.

put down

If you put down money when you are buying something, you pay a part of the money that you owe.

I had put down the first month's rent as a security deposit.

Do you want me to put a deposit down to secure the offer?

sell off

If you sell something off, you sell it to get rid of it, usually for a low price.

They plan to break up the company and sell it off.

The land was sold off to developers.

sell out

If something sells out, or if a shop sells out of it, it has all been sold.

Shops almost immediately sold out of the product.

The toy was so popular, every store in town was sold out.

set aside

If you set aside something, or you set something aside, you keep it for a particular purpose.

Set aside a fixed amount every month towards your pension.

I try to set some money aside in case of emergencies.

Some time should be set aside for preparation.

NOTE   You can also use put aside.

take out

1 If you take out something such as a licence, an insurance policy, or a bank loan, you arrange to get it.

We took out a loan to buy the car.

How much the policy pays depends on when you took it out.

2 If you take money out, you obtain it from your bank account.

You can take cash out at any ATM.

What is the best way to take out money when travelling abroad?

Exercise 1

Complete the sentences. Choose the correct particle.

1 The cost of the operation will amount *at / to / in* 165,000 Euros.
2 I've come *into / to / in* a little money. I'll be able to repay that loan sooner than expected.
3 Are you struggling to pay *over / off / down* your debts?
4 We have put *to / over / down* a deposit on a new house.
5 The company plan to sell *off / over / down* the shares next month.
6 The cash was set *around / aside / away* for road and rail improvements.

Exercise 2

Match phrasal verbs 1–6 with definitions A–F.

1 She wanted to build up her savings a bit more before she retired.
2 They got into some financial difficulties at the start of the year.
3 One supermarket sold out of the product in just one day.
4 I don't know how he manages to live on $200 a week.
5 Trina went to the bank to take out some money.
6 Kwame had put aside some cash to cover any additional costs.

A buy things that you need (with a certain amount of money)
B gradually increase the amount of something
C keep something for a particular purpose
D obtain (money) from your bank account
E reach a point where you have no more to sell
F start to be involved in something unintentionally

Exercise 3

Complete the sentences with the phrasal verbs in the box.

| pay for | added up to | brings in | taking out | sold off | cut back on |

1 I think we should consider _____ a loan to help us pay for the wedding.
2 It's better for them to _____ unnecessary expenses as much as possible.
3 Stanley didn't have enough money to _____ such an expensive car.
4 The building was _____ for very little money by the local council.
5 The total cost of the holiday _____ over ten thousand Euros.
6 Tourism _____ a lot of money to the city.

Exercise 4

Match questions 1–6 with the correct replies A–F.

1 Have you set aside any money for emergencies?
2 Is it true that he's a millionaire?
3 How much interest have you earned?
4 Would't you like to earn more money?
5 Can I pay in money electronically from one account to the other?
6 How much does roof insulation cost?

A It's quite expensive, but it should pay for itself within a year due to lower heating bills.
B No, I wouldn't. I have enough money to live on, and I'm happy with that.
C The total interest amounts to $500.
D Yes, he came into a lot of money after his father died.
E Yes, if you sign up to our Internet banking service.
F Yes. I've got some cash available to cover any unexpected costs.

Exercise 5

Complete these adverts. Write the correct particle.

1 DEBTS? WE CAN HELP YOU PAY THEM _____!
2 YOU WON'T NEED TO CUT BACK _____ LUXURY WHEN YOU SHOP WITH US.
3 YOU CAN TAKE _____ YOUR MONEY WHEN IT SUITS YOU.
4 DON'T DELAY – PUT _____ A DEPOSIT TODAY!
5 WORK FOR US AND BRING _____ MORE MONEY!
6 BUILD _____ YOUR SAVINGS WITH OUR GOLD SAVERS ACCOUNT.

Exercise 6

Correct the phrasal verbs in these sentences.

1 In order to save money, we are cutting off on unnecessary stationery.
2 It took us a while to build for a large database, but we've succeeded in that now.
3 How are you ever going to pay in all these expensive things you've bought on your credit card?
4 Having too many credit cards is a common way for people to get on debt.
5 She's come on some money and has bought a huge house in the south of France.
6 It's a good idea to set off some money for when you have retired.

Exercise 7

Make these sentences less formal. Replace the <u>underlined</u> verbs with the phrasal verbs in the box.

| built up | cut back on | give away | paying in | brings in | came into |

1 If you're going to the bank, would you mind <u>depositing</u> a cheque for me?
2 I'm going to <u>donate</u> some old clothes to a charity.
3 He <u>inherited</u> a lot of money when his wealthy grandparents died.
4 We need to <u>reduce</u> the amount of money we spend on food.
5 It's only a part-time job, but it <u>makes me</u> some extra money at least.
6 I'm saving a little money every month for my annual holiday. At the end of the year, it will have <u>grown</u> into a sizeable fund .

Exercise 8

Read this extract from a financial advice website. <u>Underline</u> all the phrasal verbs, then decide if the sentences that follow are true (*T*) or false (*F*).

MONEY MATTERS

If you're looking to put down a deposit on a house, you might think you can't afford it, but there are things you can do to help. Cutting back on luxuries you don't need is a great way to build up your savings. You might also want to consider taking out a loan to help cover the cost of a large deposit. Remember, if you do get into debt, don't worry – there are companies out there who can help you to pay it off.

1 There are things you can do to help pay for a deposit on a house. ☐
2 Spending more on luxuries can help to increase your savings. ☐
3 You should consider arranging to get a loan. ☐
4 If you start to owe a lot of money, you should worry about it. ☐
5 There are companies who can help you pay all the money that you owe. ☐

Your turn!

Look for a website that offers financial advice. Can you find any examples of the phrasal verbs in this unit?

Happy birthday Billy. Don't forget to **put** some **aside** for your pension.

HAPPY 10th BIRTHDAY!

Reporting in the media

bring about

To bring about something means to cause it to happen.

The Administration helped bring about a peaceful settlement.

We're pressing for more information on what brought the decision about.

call for

If you call for an action, you demand that it should be done.

New safety measures have been called for.

call in

If you call someone in, you ask them to come somewhere to do something for you.

The Army was called in to control the rioting.

They called him in for questioning last night.

call off

If you call off an event or an arrangement that has been planned, you cancel it.

We planned the match for yesterday afternoon but had to call it off because of the weather.

Union leaders have agreed to call off the strike.

come after

To come after a particular event, point in time or person is to happen or exist later than them.

The shock news comes after a series of incidents last month.

come under

If someone or something comes under something difficult or unpleasant from other people, they experience it.

The department has come under fire for wasting public money.

get around

If recent information gets around or gets around a place, a lot of people tell other people about it.

The news got around that he was leaving.

Gossip gets around the film industry much faster than in other places.

NOTE   You can also use get round. This is mainly British.

look for

If you look for something, you try to achieve it or get it.

We must look for a peaceful solution.

make up

If you make up something, you invent it.

He was accused of making up some of the stories in his autobiography.

She continued to talk, making it up as she went along.

meet with

1. If you meet with a particular experience or event, you experience it or it happens to you.

   Troops met with strong resistance as they entered the city.

2. If something meets with a particular reaction or if you meet something with a particular reaction, that is the reaction it gets.

   His comments met with great public approval.

   They are determined to meet any attack with retaliation.

   I told him where I was and was met with silence.

put out

To put out information means to officially tell it to many people.

The company put out a statement saying that the chief executive had resigned.

He's put the story out himself.

result from

If a situation results from an event or action, it is caused by that event or action.

The condition may result from a shortage of vitamins.

result in

If something results in a particular situation or event, it causes that situation or event to happen.

A warming of the earth's surface might result in the melting of the polar ice caps.

run through

1. If an idea, piece of news, or emotion runs through a place or a group of people, it spreads through the place or group quickly.

   A buzz of excitement ran through the crowd.

2. If a quality or feeling runs through something, it affects every part of it or is present everywhere within it.

   There is a prejudice that runs through our society.

set in

If something unpleasant sets in, it begins and seems likely to continue.

By the time he got back, panic had set in.

stem from

If something stems from something, it is caused by that thing.

Attitudes like these stem from ignorance.

step in

If you step in, you get involved in a situation and try to help.

The government sometimes has to step in to protect employees from employers.

turn into

If someone or something turns into another thing, or if something turns them into it, they change and become that other thing.

This situation is turning into a nightmare.

The novel is being turned into a television series.

Exercise 1

Complete the news headlines with the particles in the box.

IN | INTO | UNDER | OFF | FROM | WITH

1 TENNIS FINAL CALLED _____ DUE TO BAD WEATHER
2 PRESIDENT CALLS _____ ARMY TO HELP
3 GAS LEAK COULD TURN _____ DISASTER
4 WINNING TEAM MET _____ JOY ON RETURN HOME
5 JOB CUTS STEM _____ BAD DECISIONS
6 PRIME MINISTER COMES _____ PRESSURE

Exercise 2

Complete the sentences. Choose the correct particles.

1 It is hoped that the case will bring *off / about / through* some changes to the law.
2 The peaceful debate turned *up / out / into* an angry argument.
3 The Prime Minister came *under / from / in* fire from the public about his decision.
4 The call for strike action came *about / off / after* talks between the managers and the union.
5 Newspapers sometimes make *out / up / through* stories about celebrities just to catch the public's interest.
6 The government's new policies on education have been met *with / up / out* approval.

Exercise 3

Decide if the following sentences are true (*T*) or false (*F*).

1 If you bring about something, you cause it to happen. ☐
2 If you step in, you get involved in a situation and try to help. ☐
3 If you look for something, you try to achieve it. ☐
4 If something comes after an event, it happens before it. ☐
5 If something bad sets in, it begins and seems likely to continue. ☐
6 If news gets around, nobody knows about it. ☐

Exercise 4

Make these sentences sound less formal. Replace the underlined verbs with the phrasal verbs in the box.

brought about | looking for | make up | put out | runs through | step in

1 Millions of young people are now seeking work.
2 The general view that pervades this culture is that you can't come second; winning is everything.
3 The government may be forced to intervene if the dispute cannot be resolved.
4 This change was caused by the development of the Internet.
5 The police released an official statement last night.
6 Children often invent stories.

Exercise 5

Read this news story. Underline all the phrasal verbs, then match them with the correct definitions 1–6.

CITY CENTRE TRAFFIC BAN

Environmental campaigners have called for a ban on traffic in the city centre. This comes after pollution levels were found to be dangerously high for two years running. The campaigners' plans to turn the city centre into a car-free zone have met with support from city residents. Campaign spokesman Derek Shields said: 'Closing the city centre to traffic would result in lower carbon emissions and make the city a more pleasant space to live in. It's time for the city authorities to step in and address this problem.'

1 cause a situation or event to happen _____
2 get involved in a situation and try to help _____
3 happens or exists later than a particular event or point in time _____
4 change something and make it become another thing _____
5 got a particular reaction _____
6 demanded that an action should be done _____

Exercise 6

Correct the phrasal verbs in these sentences.

1 World leaders have called in action after the news of the attack.
2 Although the company hadn't made a formal announcement, word soon got through that the director had resigned.
3 A ripple of excitement ran across the football fans as their hero came on to the pitch.
4 Eventually the army had to step out and offer assistance to the flood victims.
5 Minutes after the explosion, panic set around and people began to flee the building.
6 The headmaster decided it was time to call off the police to sort out the problem of theft in the school.

Exercise 7

Match news stories A–F with headlines 1–6.

1 SMITH CRITICISES GOVERNMENT THINKING ☐
2 SCHOOL ACCUSES PUPIL OF LYING ☐
3 RETAIL SALES GETTING BETTER ☐
4 RESIDENTS REJECT BUILDING PLANS ☐
5 HIGH PRICES CAUSED BY IMPORTED FUEL ☐
6 TAX RISE WILL MAKE PEOPLE POORER ☐

A Teachers have accused the boy of making the story up to get attention.
B The increased fuel costs could result from the country's reliance on foreign fuel imports.
C Increasing taxes will only result in the poorest people becoming even less well-off.
D She said: 'This kind of thinking runs through our entire government, and it could harm our economy.'
E Plans to build the new shopping mall have come under attack from local residents.
F The survey found that sales were in fact increasing in some sectors. This comes just one month after official figures suggested a more gloomy forecast.

Exercise 8

Complete the sentences with the correct form of the phrasal verbs in the box.

meet with	call for	get round	result from	result in	call in	turn into	call off

1 The opposition leader is now _____ an independent inquiry.
2 Police from other areas were _____ to assist with the boat rescue.
3 The singer may be forced to _____ next week's concert due to illness.
4 Last week, a story _____ that the manager had stolen company funds.
5 The judge's comments were _____ outrage from the public.
6 She was afraid of the damage to the company that would _____ such a scandal.
7 The accident _____ several injuries.
8 The problem of child obesity is threatening to _____ a public health disaster.

Your turn!

Look at news stories that interest you in a newspaper or online. Can you find any examples of the phrasal verbs in this unit?

Critics say the match should have been **called off.**

Political events

bring down

If people or events bring down a government or ruler, they cause them to lose their power.

Unofficial strikes had brought down the regime.

A national strike would bring the government down.

bring in

When a government or other organization brings in a new law, rule, or system, they introduce it.

We intend to bring in legislation to control their activities.

The government should bring laws in to restrict the sale of unhealthy food.

crack down

To crack down is to start to be much stricter with people who are not obeying rules or laws, punishing them more severely.

Their first reaction to the riots was to crack down hard.

NOTE   You can also use clamp down.

deal with

When you deal with something that needs attention, you do what is necessary in order to achieve the result that is wanted.

They learned to deal with any sort of emergency.

engage in

If you engage in an activity, you take part in it.

It was not considered appropriate for a former President to engage in business.

They were engaged in a life and death struggle.

enter into

1 If you enter into an agreement or arrangement, you formally agree to it.

His party entered into an alliance with the Socialists.

2 If you enter into an activity, you start it or become involved in it.

The government refused to enter into negotiations.

fight back

If you fight back when someone or something attacks you or causes you problems, you defend yourself and try to beat them or stop them.

Our troops were fighting back desperately.

force into

If you force someone into doing something, you make them do it, although they do not want to.

They are trying to force their employers into increasing their wages.

go ahead

When someone goes ahead with something which they planned or asked permission to do, they begin to do it, and when a plan goes ahead, it begins.

They are going ahead with the project.

The meeting is going ahead as planned.

impose on

If you impose something on people, you use your authority to force them to accept it.

The United Nations has imposed sanctions on the country.

The rule was imposed on small businesses.

NOTE   You can also use impose upon.

lead to

If something leads to a situation or event, usually an unpleasant one, it causes it.

He warned yesterday that pay increases would lead to job losses.

pull out

If soldiers or an army pull out or if someone pulls them out, they leave a place.

Troops have begun to pull out of the area.

The Prime Minister has said he intends to pull all 10,000 soldiers out by the end of June.

The government has pulled out the army.

push for

If you push for something, you try to persuade other people to help you achieve it.

Unions were pushing for higher wages.

NOTE   You can also use press for.

sort out

If you sort something out, you solve a problem, misunderstanding, or disagreement.

It could take months to sort this mess out.

Officials from both sides are meeting today to sort out their differences.

Once this issue has sorted itself out, we'll be ready to start.

stand by

If you stand by, you allow something bad to happen without trying to do anything to stop it.

We cannot stand by and watch while our allies are attacked.

NOTE   You can also use sit by.

stand for

1 If a letter stands for a particular word or name, it is an abbreviation for that word or name.

EU stands for European Union.

2 If someone stands for something, they are a candidate in an election.

No one would stand for election.

Exercise 1

Match the particles with the verbs to make phrasal verbs from this unit.

| down | for | out | ahead | in | into | back | by |

1 stand / sit   _____
2 fight   _____
3 bring / crack / clamp _____
4 bring / engage   _____

5 push / press / stand   _____
6 enter / force   _____
7 go   _____
8 pull / sort   _____

Exercise 2

Complete the sentences. Choose the correct particles.

1 You can't ignore the situation much longer, You are going to have to deal *by / with / in* it.
2 We had no choice in the matter. The rules were imposed *for / into / on* us.
3 We've decided to go *back / ahead / down* with the plans to develop the business.
4 The management and the union have entered *on / over / into* negotiations over pensions.
5 The race has been cancelled. Several of the athletes have had to pull *out / off / away* because of ill health.
6 Does the abbreviation E.C. stand *by / for / over* European Commission or European Community?

Exercise 3

Match phrasal verbs 1–8 with definitions A–H.

1 They would support military action to bring down the regime.
2 The government wants to clamp down on crime.
3 Health professionals are now engaged in discussions.
4 They are refusing to enter into any kind of negotiations.
5 We must fight back against corruption.
6 The campaign was designed to force the Government into a referendum on the issue.
7 Military action is not the way to sort out this problem.
8 We must push the Government for action.

A take part in
B start or become involved in an activity
C cause a government or ruler to lose their power
D make someone do something when they do not want to
E start to be much stricter with people who are not obeying laws
F try to persuade other people to help you achieve something
G solve a problem, misunderstanding, or disagreement
H defend yourself and try to stop someone who attacks you

Exercise 4

Complete the headlines with the particles in the box.

| BACK | IN | DOWN | BY | INTO | AHEAD |

1 POLICE CRACK _____ ON CRIME
2 EU COUNTRIES TO ENTER _____ NEW AGREEMENT
3 STUDENTS FIGHT _____ AGAINST INCREASE IN COLLEGE FEES
4 HEALTH CARE REFORMS TO GO _____ NEXT YEAR
5 ENVIRONMENT MINISTER STANDS _____ HER VIEWS ON CLIMATE CHANGE
6 GOVERNMENT TO BRING _____ NEW LAW AGAINST FRAUD

Exercise 5

Complete the sentences with the phrasal verbs in the box.

| bring in | dealing with | engage in | pull … out | lead to | imposed … on |

1 Authorities are now _____ the situation.
2 At that time, the government _____ restrictions _____ imports to protect the economy.
3 There is a possibility that the dispute could _____ war.
4 The government may _____ tough new laws to combat criminals.
5 The prime minister will _____ talks with the president during a three-day tour of the country.
6 Italy may decide to _____ troops _____ from the region.

Exercise 6

Make these sentences sound less formal. Replace the <u>underlined</u> verbs with the phrasal verbs in the box.

sort out | pulled out | go ahead | fight back | bring in | bring down

1 The militia responded by saying it would <u>retaliate</u> against any attacks.
2 The company said it could not <u>proceed</u> with the plan until public confidence had been restored.
3 He said he would work with anyone who wanted to <u>resolve</u> the conflict.
4 Many people would prefer to see the troops <u>withdrawn</u>.
5 The reason for sending in the troops was to <u>topple</u> a very nasty dictator and make the world a safer place.
6 The government will <u>introduce</u> the new laws next month.

Exercise 7

Correct the phrasal verbs in these sentences.

1 We're cracking over hard on vigilante groups in general.
2 The new measures are designed to deal on immigration more effectively.
3 The agreement will lead with better relationships between the two countries.
4 The government will not stand over and allow thieves to operate in this way.
5 NATO stands on North Atlantic Treaty Organization.
6 Campaigners are pressing out a review of the current law.
7 The state dominates the groups and imposes its directives under them.
8 The two countries are engaged out a border dispute.

Exercise 8

Read this comment from a political blog. <u>Underline</u> all the phrasal verbs, then in your own words, explain what each one means.

I entered into politics because I wanted to help shape the future of my country. As a politician, I see it as my job to push for change. But I don't want to impose changes upon anyone. I want to encourage people to engage in the political process, not to just stand by and watch it happening. That's why I'm standing for Governor of this city.

1 _____   4 _____
2 _____   5 _____
3 _____   6 _____

Your turn!

Look for articles about political events in a newspaper or online. Can you find any examples of the phrasal verbs in this unit?

Entering into the agreement was easy.

Crime

break in

If someone breaks in, they get into a building illegally or by force.

A thief broke in and forced open the locked safe in the library.

The police broke in and arrested all the men.

break into

If someone breaks into a room or a building, they enter it illegally or by force.

He broke into a shop one night and stole some food.

get away

When someone or something gets away, they escape.

The police followed the gang but they got away.

get away with

If you get away with something that you should not have done, you are not criticized or punished for doing it.

No one should get away with such a crime.

get off

If you get off when you have done something wrong, or if someone gets you off, you are not punished or receive only a small punishment for what you have done.

She was sure that she would not get off so easily.

He hired a good lawyer who could get him off.

give up

1. If you give yourself up, you allow yourself to be arrested or captured.

He went straight to the local police station and gave himself up.

2. To give someone up who is wanted by the police means to tell the police where that person is so that they can be arrested.

They questioned her forcefully, but still she wouldn't give me up.

hand in

1. If you hand something in, you give it to someone in authority.

She handed the money in, thinking it was probably stolen.

Someone handed in my phone after finding it on the bus.

2. If you hand yourself in, you go to the police and tell them that you have committed a crime.

He walked into a police station and handed himself in.

hold up

To hold someone or something up means to rob them by threatening them with a weapon.

They held up a bank with sawn-off shotguns.

He held me up at gun point.

let out

If you let people or animals out, you allow them to leave a place, especially by opening a door.

The prisoners were let out of their cells for an hour a day.

We let out the dogs so that they could get some exercise.

lock in

If you lock someone in or lock them in a place, you put them somewhere and lock the door so that they cannot get out.

She pushed me into a room and locked me in.

They locked in the prisoners for the night.

The prisoners were locked in their cells for 23 hours a day.

pay for

If someone pays for something bad that they have done, they suffer or are punished because of it.

He must pay for all the crimes for which he is responsible.

resort to

If you resort to doing something that you do not think is right or acceptable, you do it because you cannot see any other way of achieving what you want.

He had resorted to stealing to feed his children.

rip off

If someone rips you off, they cheat you by charging you too much money for something. [INFORMAL]

The local shopkeepers were all trying to rip off the tourists.

The court wastes my time and the lawyers rip me off!

run away

1 If you run away, you leave a place or person by running.

The thief then ran away and jumped into a car.

2 If you run away, you secretly leave a place because you are unhappy.

When she was sixteen, she had an argument with her parents and ran away from home.

take in

1 If the police take you in, they make you go with them to a police station in order to ask you questions or arrest you.

The police took him in for questioning.

2 If you are taken in by someone or if they take you in, they deceive or trick you.

I gave him the money before I realized I had been taken in.

I confess he completely took me in.

track down

If you track down someone or something, you find them after searching for some time.

The FBI is putting a lot of effort into tracking down the criminals.

Soon the police tracked Charles down and arrested him.

NOTE   You can also use hunt down

Exercise 1

Match the particles with the verbs to make phrasal verbs from this unit.

off | in | away | up

1 break / hand / lock / take ____
2 get / run   ____
3 give / hold   ____
4 get / rip   ____

Exercise 2

Complete the sentences. Choose the correct particle.

1 Thieves managed to break *at / to / in* and steal thousands of dollars.
2 Fire fighters had to break *into / onto / over* the house to reach the family.
3 Erik said he would never give himself *on / out / up* to the police.
4 Carlos went to the nearest police station and handed the money *on / in / into*.
5 A bank was held *up / out / in* yesterday by three masked men.
6 He paid *over / under / for* his crime with twenty years in prison.
7 Evans managed to run *with / away / into* before the police arrived.
8 We are working hard to track *down / out / up* these cyber criminals.

Exercise 3

Decide if the following sentences are true (*T*) or false (*F*).

1 If someone gets away, they escape. ☐
2 If you get off when you have done something wrong, you are punished severely. ☐
3 If you let someone out, you allow them to leave a place. ☐
4 If you lock someone in, you put them somewhere and lock the door. ☐
5 If you resort to doing something that you do not think is right, you do it because you cannot see any other way of achieving what you want. ☐
6 If someone rips you off, they do not charge you any money for something. ☐
7 If you hunt down someone, you find them after searching for some time. ☐
8 If the police take you in, they allow you to leave a place. ☐

Exercise 4

Match sentence halves 1–8 with A–H to make complete sentences.

1 How did the robbers   A decided to give himself up.
2 You will never get away   B out of prison?
3 After several hours, the gunman   C these crimes with a long prison sentence.
4 The man held   D sold you the car ripped you off.
5 Do you think they will ever be let   E manage to break in?
6 He may have to pay for   F to crime to make money.
7 They say they were forced to resort   G with this crime!
8 I think the man who   H up a department store yesterday afternoon.

Exercise 5

Complete the sentences with the phrasal verbs in the box.

got away | handed ... in | running away | locked ... in | broke into | get ... off

1 Someone _____ the office and stole the computer.
2 The boys _____ before she had a chance to call the police.
3 His lawyer said that given the seriousness of the crime, it would not be easy to _____ him _____.
4 She found a purse and _____ it _____ to the hotel reception.
5 The sheriff _____ him _____ a cell overnight.
6 He hated his stepfather and thought about _____ from home.

Exercise 6

Match phrasal verbs 1–6 with a word or phrase A–F with the same meaning.

1 She was taken in by the criminal's persuasive tactics.
2 The thief decided to give himself up to the police.
3 I can't believe he got away with such dishonesty.
4 The police managed to track down the robbers.
5 Be careful – they always try to rip off tourists in the main square.
6 After a short time in prison, he was let out.

A cheat
B find
C fooled
D set free
E surrender
F wasn't caught or punished for

Exercise 7

Complete the news headlines. Write the correct particle.

1 WOMAN TAKEN _____ BY FRAUDSTER
2 BANKS ARE RIPPING _____ THEIR CUSTOMERS
3 THIEF WILL PAY _____ CRIME, IN JAIL
4 FATHER GIVES _____ SON TO POLICE
5 DANGEROUS CRIMINAL HUNTED _____ BY LOCAL POLICE
6 BOY, 14, RUNS _____ FROM HOME

Exercise 8

Read the news report. <u>Underline</u> all the phrasal verbs, then answer the questions.

A man who held up a bank in the city centre has been arrested by police. The man locked staff in a store room while he attempted to break into the safe. When the safe would not open, he tried to run away. But police arrived in time to stop him. Police chief Dean Sanchez said: 'He was foolish to think he could get away with this.' Three other men have been taken in for questioning.

1 What did the man try to rob?
2 Why could staff not leave the store room?
3 What did he try to enter illegally?
4 Why did he try to leave?
5 What was the man foolish to think?
6 How many other men have police taken to the police station?

Your turn!

Look for news stories about crime in a newspaper or online. Can you find any examples of the phrasal verbs in this unit?

It didn't take long to **track down** the criminal.

24

Disaster and destruction

blow away

☐ If something blows away or if the wind blows it away, the wind moves it away from the place where it was.

There was a massive storm one night and our shed blew away.

The wind blew his papers away.

My hat was blown away.

blow up

If you blow something up or if it blows up, it is destroyed by an explosion.

He was going to blow the place up.

The gunmen were threatening to blow up the embassy.

One of the submarines blew up and sank.

break down

☐ When a machine or a vehicle breaks down, it stops working.

His car broke down on the motorway.

☐ To break down something such as a door or wall means to hit it hard so that it breaks and falls to the ground.

Water had flooded their homes and broken down the walls.

Police broke the door down.

NOTE   You can also use smash down.

break out

If something unpleasant breaks out, it begins suddenly.

A fire broke out on the third floor.

cut off

☐ If a person or place is cut off, they are separated from other people and places.

The town was cut off by the floods.

☐ To cut off the supply of something means to stop it.

The hurricane cut off electricity to at least 3.5 million people.

Gas supplies have now been cut off.

fall down

☐ If someone or something falls down when they have been in an upright position, they drop to the ground.

A tree fell down during the storm.

☐ If something such as a building or bridge falls down, it breaks into pieces because it is old, weak, or damaged.

That shelter might fall down if the rain comes back.

go off

If a gun goes off, it is fired and if a bomb goes off, it explodes.

Somebody's gun went off by mistake.

knock out

1 To knock someone out means to cause them to become unconscious or to fall asleep.

The explosion hurt no one, except that it knocked out Colonel Lacour.

He must have fallen and knocked himself out.

NOTE   The opposite of knock out is bring round.

2 To knock something out means to destroy or damage it and stop it from working properly.

A huge storm had knocked all the power out.

Lightning knocked out the city's power grid.

put out

If you put out something that is burning, you cause it to stop burning.

He put the fire out.

The fire was put out very quickly.

reduce to

If something, especially a building or a city, is reduced to a state where it is broken or destroyed or if someone reduces it to this state, someone or something breaks or destroys it.

Every building in the town was reduced to rubble.

The fire reduced the house to dust.

run out

1 If you run out of something, you have no more of it left.

We were rapidly running out of medical supplies.

2 If something runs out, it becomes used up so that there is no more left.

There was no water, and food was running out.

run over

If a vehicle or its driver runs over someone or something, the vehicle hits them or drives over them, causing injury or damage.

We almost ran over a cat that was crossing the road.

I'm sure he would have run us over.

NOTE   You can also use run down and knock down.

wipe out

To wipe someone or something out means to destroy or get rid of them completely.

Epidemics wiped out the local population.

Illegal hunting could wipe the animals out.

write off

If someone writes off a vehicle or other machine, they damage it so badly that it is not worth repairing. [BRITISH]

She had crashed the car twice, writing it off completely the second time.

He wrote off the car and left a passenger with two broken legs.

Exercise 1

Complete the news headlines with the particles in the box.

TO | DOWN | OUT | OFF | OUT | UP

1 BUS BREAKS _____ CAUSING TRAFFIC JAM
2 MALFUNCTION CAUSES POWER PLANT TO BLOW _____
3 POWER CUT _____ FOR THOUSANDS OF CITY RESIDENTS
4 BRIDGE REDUCED _____ RUBBLE IN TRAIN CRASH
5 MILLIONS COULD BE WIPED _____ BY DISEASE
6 FIREFIGHTERS STRUGGLE TO PUT _____ BLAZE

Exercise 2

Match phrasal verbs 1–8 with definitions A–H.

1 Some tents were blown away in the storm.
2 The fire broke out on the fifteenth floor.
3 An earthquake caused the buildings to fall down.
4 A bomb went off in the building last night.
5 The fumes from the fire knocked her out for a short time.
6 We need to use less water, otherwise we might run out.
7 He was run over by a bus and injured.
8 The car was completely written off in the accident.

A hit or drive over someone, causing injury
B have no more of something left
C explode
D damage a vehicle so it is not worth repairing
E cause someone to become unconscious
F break into pieces due to being old, weak, or damaged
G begin suddenly
H be moved away from a place by the wind

Exercise 3

Make these sentences less formal. Replace the underlined verbs with the phrasal verbs in the box.

put out | run out | blew up | smash down | wipe out | going off

1 They had to demolish the door to get access to the apartment.
2 It took them four hours to extinguish the fire.
3 Scientists are trying to eradicate the disease.
4 A car was destroyed in the explosion.
5 Police managed to stop the bomb exploding last night.
6 The town's food supplies are starting to decrease.

Exercise 4

Match questions 1–8 with replies A–H.

1 Who was injured in the explosion?
2 When did the war break out?
3 Was this area affected by the floods?
4 What kind of damage was caused by the earthquake?
5 Did you lose your power supply during the storm?
6 What happened to the building during the hurricane?
7 Was there an accident on this road earlier?
8 Did you write off your car in the accident?

A Yes, the storm knocked out our electricity.
B Many buildings fell down as a result of it.
C Yes, someone was knocked down by a car.
D No one was injured. But a car was blown up.
E It started about a year ago.
F Yes, the flood water completely cut off parts of the town.
G No, but the other car was badly damaged.
H It was completely reduced to rubble.

Exercise 5

Correct the phrasal verbs in these sentences.

1 The wind blew up all the papers on my desk.
2 My car broke out on the way to work.
3 After the petrol shortage, petrol supplies have all run down.
4 The earthquake caused large parts of the building to fall through.
5 It took fire fighters several days to put off the fire.
6 She wrote away the car when she crashed into a wall.

Exercise 6

Complete the sentences with the correct form of the phrasal verbs in the box.

run down | go off | break down | blow up | blow away | reduce to

1 Hundreds were left homeless after storms _____ their houses.
2 The boat was _____ fifty years ago by a torpedo.
3 Last night the train _____ leaving passengers stuck for eight hours.
4 The old wooden shed was _____ a pile of wood by the storm.
5 She thought she could hear the sound of a gun _____ in the distance.
6 A man was _____ by a bus while trying to cross the road.

Exercise 7

Choose the best answers.

1 What breaks out?
   A a fire   B the wind   C a car
2 What usually blows something away?
   A an explosion   B the wind   C a balloon
3 What breaks down?
   A a building   B a vehicle   C a tree
4 What falls down during a storm?
   A a road   B the wind   C a tree
5 What can be written off?
   A a letter   B a building   C a car
6 What can be put out?
   A fire   B war   C an explosion

Exercise 8

Read the news story. <u>Underline</u> all the phrasal verbs, then decide if the sentences that follow are true (*T*) or false (*F*).

FOREST FIRES UNDER CONTROL

A forest fire that broke out on a farm three days ago is now under control. Firefighters were running out of water supplies yesterday, but helicopters brought extra supplies today to help put out the blaze. Huge areas of forest have been wiped out by the fire. Many farm buildings were also reduced to rubble. Fortunately the fire did not spread to a nearby town, which could have cut the town off from firefighters.

1 The fire started on a farm. ☐
2 Firefighters did not have enough water supplies yesterday. ☐
3 They have still not stopped the fire burning. ☐
4 Large areas of forest were destroyed by the fire. ☐
5 No buildings were damaged. ☐
6 A nearby town was separated from the firefighters by the fire. ☐

Your turn!

Look for news stories about an accident or disaster in a newspaper or online. Can you find any examples of the phrasal verbs in this unit?

Putting out the fire wasn't a problem.

25

Helping and recovering

carry on

1. If you carry on, you continue doing an activity.

   We are determined to carry on with our work.

   NOTE   You can also use go on.

2. If you carry on when you are in a difficult or unpleasant situation, you manage to continue with your normal, everyday activities.

   Some people carry on as if nothing has happened.

   NOTE   You can also use go on.

clean up

1. If you clean up something that is dirty or untidy, you get rid of it by wiping, sweeping, etc.

   Anne cleaned up the house and sat at the kitchen table.

2. If you clean up or clean up a place or person, you clean them.

   Consider for a moment the costs of cleaning up rivers and beaches.

   NOTE   You can also use clear up.

get through

1. If you get through a task, you succeed in finishing it.

   I got though a lot of work this morning.

2. If you get through a difficult experience, or someone or something gets you through it, you survive it.

   I just have to get through the next few months and then it'll be fine.

help out

If you help out or help someone out, you do something to help someone.

My sister helps out with the kids a lot.

hold on

1. If you hold on, you hold something firmly, especially to stop yourself from falling.

   I grabbed the railing and held on.

2. If you hold on, you manage to continue in a difficult situation.

   If you hold on, things will get better eventually.

   NOTE   The opposite of hold on is give up.

hold on to

1. If you hold on to something that is in your hand, you grip it tightly so that it cannot fall or cannot be taken away from you.

   She walked slowly down the steps, holding on to the hand-rail.

   NOTE   You can also use hold onto.

2. If you hold on to someone, you keep your arms around them.

   She held on to him for support.

   NOTE   You can also use hold onto.

keep on

If you keep on, or keep on doing something, you continue doing something and do not stop.

My hands were shaking but I kept on.

I kept on running until I had reached the house.

NOTE   You can also use carry on.

look after

If you look after someone or something, you take care of them and make sure they have what they need.

My mother looks after the baby during the week.

leave behind

If you leave something behind, you stop having a past feeling or experience and progress to something new.

This is your chance to leave the past behind and make a new start.

It can be hard to leave behind these bad experiences.

live with

If you have to live with something unpleasant, you have to accept it and carry on with your life or work.

The job involved a lot of stress, but I learnt to live with it.

NOTE   You can also use put up with. This is more informal.

protect from

To protect someone or something from something bad or harmful means to prevent it from happening or having a harmful effect.

The soldiers were there to protect their country from invasion.

Make sure you cover up and protect yourself from the sun.

NOTE   You can also use protect against.

settle down

If something settles down, it becomes calmer or stops changing.

When things settle down a bit you'll have to come and visit us.

NOTE   You can also use calm down.

take in

If you take someone in, you allow them to live at your house or in your country.

After the hurricane, neighbours offered to take homeless families in.

Governments in the region may have to take in large numbers of refugees.

turn around

If someone or something turns your life around or if it turns around, it changes completely, usually becoming better.

An opportunity like this could turn your entire life around.

The organization helps people turn around their lives.

My life turned around when I met Tom.

Exercise 1

Match the particles with the verbs to make phrasal verbs from this unit.

| down | out | from | in | on | up | around | with |

1 carry / hold / keep / go _____
2 clear / clean _____
3 help _____
4 protect _____

5 live _____
6 settle _____
7 turn _____
8 take _____

Exercise 2

Match sentence halves 1–6 with A–F to make complete definitions.

1 If you clean up a place or person,

2 If you hold on to someone,
3 If you leave something behind,
4 If you look after someone or something,
5 If something settles down,
6 If you take someone in,

A you stop having a past feeling and progress to something new.
B you take care of them.
C you make them cleaner.
D it becomes calmer or stops changing.
E you allow them to live at your house or in your country.
F you keep your arms around them.

Exercise 3

Decide if the sentences are true (*T*) or false (*F*).

1 If something turns your life around, it changes your life for the worse. ☐
2 If you look after something, you ignore it. ☐
3 If something gets you through a difficult situation, it helps you cope. ☐
4 If you carry on in a difficult situation, you stop living your life normally. ☐
5 If things settle down, they become calmer. ☐
6 If you hold on to something, you give it to someone else. ☐

Exercise 4

Complete the book titles with the particles in the box.

| BEHIND | WITH | AROUND | OUT | FROM | AFTER |

1 HOW TO TURN YOUR LIFE _____
2 LEAVING YOUR PAST _____
3 LOOKING _____ YOUR NEW BABY
4 LIVING _____ STRESS
5 PROTECTING YOURSELF _____ HARM
6 HELPING _____: A GUIDE TO CHARITY WORK

Exercise 5

Replace the <u>underlined</u> verbs with a phrasal verb from the box with the same meaning.

| settled down | live with | kept on | held on to | clean up | protect ... from |

1 It took us hours to <u>clear up</u> the mess the children had made.
2 You need to take measures to <u>protect</u> yourself <u>against</u> skin cancer.
3 Qiang doesn't like going to the dentist, but he can <u>put up with</u> it.
4 She <u>held onto</u> his hand as they walked up the hill.
5 I <u>carried on</u> walking along the street.
6 Life has <u>calmed down</u> more now that we've moved away from the city.

Exercise 6

Correct the phrasal verbs in these sentences.

1 It was difficult for him to carry in after the accident.
2 I just don't know how we're going to get ahead this difficult time.
3 If there's anything I can do to help in, just let me know.
4 Things will get better – You just need to keep holding over!
5 Dario really wanted to leave his past ahead and move on with life.
6 I offered to look under Helen's children while she's in hospital.
7 After a few hours, his stomach settled over and he ate a sandwich.
8 They took at a homeless couple for a week while they looked for a place to stay.

Exercise 7

Read Oliver's story. <u>Underline</u> all the phrasal verbs, then match them with definitions 1–6.

When I was younger, I was homeless and had nowhere to go. I became depressed. Then I met Sophie and that turned my life around. We became friends and she took me in and let me live in her house. She looked after me and even helped me out with things like money. She helped me get through my depression and now I really feel like I've left that part of my life behind.

1 stopped having a past feeling and progressed to something new
2 took care of me
3 survive something
4 did something to help me
5 changed my life completely and made it better
6 allowed me to live at her house

Exercise 8

Complete the sentences with the correct forms of phrasal verbs from this unit.

1 If I can find someone to _____ my baby tonight, I can come to the cinema with you.
2 I hope you'll be happy in your new home! When you've unpacked and things have _____, I'd love to come and visit.
3 When you're climbing up the mountain, _____ the rope tightly.
4 The post office is just ahead of you, at the end of this street. Just _____ and you'll see it, on your right.
5 It was a great party – but the room is a mess! It'll take us a long time to _____. We'd better start now.
6 When our son left home to go to university, we _____ a lodger. It helped pay the rent and made the house feel less empty without him.

Your turn!

Can you think of someone or something that has helped you at some time in your life? Use the phrasal verbs in this unit to talk about them. For example:

My sister looked after me when I was sick.

The book helped me get through a difficult time in my life.

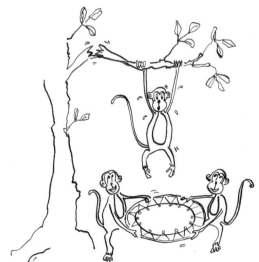

He knew his friends would **get** him **through** this ordeal.

Appendix 1   Learning phrasal verbs

There are lots of things you can do to make learning and remembering phrasal verbs easier. Below are some tips to help you do this.

Learning phrasal verbs as single units of meaning

While phrasal verbs are combinations of two or three words, it is helpful when you are learning them to think about them as single units of meaning.

phrasal verb	meaning
opt for	decide to do or have a particular thing
cut back on	reduce the money that you spend on something
talk into	persuade someone to do something

Using phrasal verbs in full sentences

If you write down full sentences containing the phrasal verb this will help you remember what it means and how to use it correctly. The example sentences given in this book will help you see clearly how a phrasal verb is used.

phrasal verb	full sentence example
opt for	*Unsure what to study at university, she eventually opted for Law.*
cut back on	*The government has had to cut back on public spending.*
talk into	*She talked me into taking a week's holiday.*

Grouping phrasal verbs by topic

Learning phrasal verbs by topic, as they are arranged in this book, will help you remember them. When you are making a note of phrasal verbs, it may be helpful to group them under topics that relate to your own life, for example your job or your personal interests.

phrasal verb	topic
opt for	Studying and learning
cut back on	Money and spending
talk into	Discussions

Remembering phrasal verbs with images or stories

A good way to help you remember a phrasal verb is to imagine an image or story that illustrates it. For example, the phrasal verb *step down* means to leave an important job or position. To help you remember this, you could imagine a company boss standing above all the workers on a stepladder, and then stepping down onto the floor and walking away.

Identifying phrasal verbs in context

Look out for phrasal verbs when you are:

* reading a book or article
* watching a film or TV programme
* looking at a website.

Pay attention to how the phrasal verb is used and in what kind of situation. Make a note about this to help you remember the right context in which to use the phrasal verb.

Appendix 2   Understanding common particles

A phrasal verb is a combination of a verb and at least one particle. Understanding some of the basic meanings of particles can help you to understand the meanings of phrasal verbs. Some common particles are *up, down, on, off, in, out, away, back, for, from, into, over, through* and *with*. Below you will find the basic meanings of these common particles, with examples of phrasal verbs from this book.

particle	AWAY		
meaning	moving to a different place	transferring or taking something to a different place	getting rid of or destroying something
example	• go **away** • get **away** • run **away**	• give **away** • take **away**	• blow **away** • throw **away**

particle	BACK	
meaning	returning to a place where you were before	controlling or suppressing something
example	• come **back** • go **back** • turn **back**	• cut **back** on • hold **back**

particle	FOR		
meaning	to state a reason, cause, purpose, or aim		
example	• go **for** • head **for** • hope **for** • try **for**	• look **for** • make **for** • opt **for** • stand **for**	• ask **for** • call **for** • care **for** • plan **for**

particle	FROM	
meaning	to talk about sources or origins	separating or preventing
example	• come **from** • result **from** • hear **from**	• keep **from** • protect **from**

particle	IN	OUT
meaning	entering or arriving at a place	leaving a place
example	• check **in** • move **in** • come **in**	• walk **out** • check **out** • get **out**
particle	IN	OUT
meaning	being involved and active	excluding, preventing or removing
example	• join **in** • step **in** • engage **in**	• pull **out** • talk **out** of • keep **out**
particle	IN	OUT
meaning	remaining somewhere, especially at home	locations outside and away from home
example	• eat **in** • stay **in** • stop **in**	• eat **out** • go **out** • hang **out**

particle	INTO	
meaning	involvement in an activity	persuading and forcing someone
example	• look **into** • get **into** • enter **into**	• force **into** • talk **into**

particle	ON	OFF
meaning	movement into something or somewhere	movement out of or away from something or somewhere
example	• get **on** • call **on** • come **on**	• get **off** • go **off** • set **off**
particle	ON	OFF
meaning	adding or attaching something	removing or disposing of something you no longer need or want
example	• put **on** • try **on** • have **on**	• take **off** • pull **off** • pay **off**
particle	ON	OFF
meaning	continuing to do something	stopping or cancelling something
example	• carry **on** • hold **on** • keep **on**	• call **off** • switch **off** • turn **off**

particle	OVER	
meaning	moving across a surface	changing or transferring something
example	• come **over** • go **over** • pull **over**	• hand **over** • take **over** • win **over**

particle	THROUGH	
meaning	passing from one side of something to another	completing something
example	• come **through**	• get **through** • go **through** • run **through**

particle	UP	DOWN
meaning	movement from a lower position or place to a higher one	movement from a higher position or place to a lower one
example	• get **up** • move **up** • stand **up**	• fall **down** • lay **down** • sit **down**
particle	UP	DOWN
meaning	an increase in size, amount, or intensity	a decrease in size, amount, or intensity
example	• grow **up** • build **up** • speed **up**	• go **down** • calm **down** • slow **down**
particle	UP	DOWN
meaning	something is starting or being prepared	something is collapsing, being cut, or destroyed
example	• get **up** • start **up** • set **up**	• knock **down** • break **down** • smash **down**

particle	WITH	
meaning	connections, associations, or relationships	supporting something
example	• deal with • finish with	• agree with • stick with

Appendix 3   Common nouns used with phrasal verbs

There are certain nouns which are commonly used together with certain phrasal verbs. It can be helpful to make a note of these as you come across them. You will find lots of examples of these in this book, in the examples given after each phrasal verb meaning. Some common noun and phrasal verb collocations are given below. Note that it is often necessary to add an article (*a/an* or *the*) between the phrasal verb and the noun, for example: *bring about <u>an</u> improvement; call off <u>the</u> strike; carry out <u>an</u> investigation.*

phrasal verb	noun collocations	examples
bring about	• change • improvement • peace • reform	New medication **brought about** a great <u>improvement</u> in her condition. Having children **brings about** huge <u>changes</u> for any couple.
call off	• search • strike • protest • visit	Union leaders have agreed to **call off** the <u>strike</u>. He has **called off** his <u>visit</u> to Texas.
carry out	• examination • experiment • investigation • search	Experts are **carrying out** an <u>investigation</u> into the accident. Officers **carried out** a <u>search</u> of all the cells.
come under	• attack • criticism • pressure • strain	Her policies have **come under** a lot of <u>criticism</u>. He **came under** a lot of <u>pressure</u> to resign.
come up with	• answer • suggestion • excuse • theory	Every week he **comes up with** a new <u>excuse</u> for being late. She **came up with** a good <u>theory</u> about why these children are hard to teach.
deal with	• issue • problem • incident • complaint	My job is to **deal with** <u>complaints</u> from customers. Police were called to **deal with** the <u>incident</u>.
enter into	• agreement • alliance • arrangement • partnership	They **entered into** a long-term <u>agreement</u> to rent the property. His party **entered into** an <u>alliance</u> with the socialists.
face up to	• truth • fact • reality • responsibility	He decided to return home and **face up to** his <u>responsibilities</u>. I had to **face up to** the <u>fact</u> that I might never see him again.
find out	• truth • answer • information • cause	We eventually **found out** the <u>truth</u> about what happened. Where can I **find out** the <u>information</u> I need?

phrasal verb	noun collocations	examples
get over	• shock • death • disappointment • surprise	*He never **got over** the <u>death</u> of his wife.* *She didn't win, but she **got over** her <u>disappointment</u> fairly quickly.*
lay off	• employee • staff • worker	*We were forced to **lay off** <u>staff</u>.* *The factory has **laid off** half its <u>workers</u>.*
make up	• bulk • majority • rest • proportion	*Household waste **makes up** a small <u>proportion</u> of the total.* *Family law **makes up** the <u>bulk</u> of my work.*
pass on	• message • tip • information • knowledge	*David **passed on** your <u>message</u> to me.* *We **passed on** all the <u>information</u> we had to the police.*
pay off	• money • debt • loan • mortgage	*We used the money to **pay off** our <u>debts</u>.* *We soon **paid off** the <u>loan</u>.*
put forward	• idea • proposal • argument • suggestion	*They **put forward** a <u>proposal</u> to build a new bridge.* *She **put forward** the <u>argument</u> that torture is wrong in any circumstance.*
sell off	• assets • land • property • business	*They were forced to **sell off** most of their <u>assets</u>.* *We **sold off** our <u>business</u>.*
set up	• business • company • commission • meeting	*He has plans to **set up** his own <u>business</u>.* *The government has **set up** a <u>commission</u> to investigate the affair.*
take out	• mortgage • loan • insurance • lease	*We **took out** a <u>loan</u> to buy the car.* *She **took out** a <u>lease</u> on a building in the city centre.*
work out	• compromise • solution • details • arrangement	*There was disagreement over the money, but eventually they **worked out** a <u>compromise</u>.* *We **worked out** an <u>arrangement</u> to cover the holiday period.*

Answer key

1 Basic actions

Exercise 1

1 E	3 B	5 D
2 C	4 A	

Exercise 2

1 back	3 back	5 on
2 in	4 into	6 in

Exercise 3

1 D	3 E	5 B
2 C	4 F	6 A

Exercise 4

1 D	3 B
2 A	4 D

Exercise 5

1 sat down	4 laid the book down
2 stood up	5 ran out
3 got up	6 get out

Exercise 6

1 got out	4 moving up
2 get up	5 laid (it) down
3 ran in	6 got off

Exercise 7

1 turn back	4 go back
2 go into	5 get up
3 move down	6 sit down

Exercise 8

SKI SAFELY!

- You must always <u>sit down</u> while using the chairlift.
- If you <u>fall down</u> on the slope, or if you fall from the chairlift, do not <u>get up</u> too quickly.
- If you fall from the chair lift, <u>keep</u> your head <u>down</u> until it is safe to <u>stand up</u> again.
- If you think you may be injured, <u>lay</u> your skis <u>down</u> on the ground and wait for help.
- Always stay with another person. Do not <u>go off</u> on your own.
- If it starts to snow heavily, you should consider <u>turning back</u>.

1 F	4 T
2 F	5 F
3 F	6 F

2 Actions with an object

Exercise 1

1 D	3 B	5 E
2 F	4 A	6 C

Exercise 2

1 up	4 at	7 down
2 back	5 on	8 up
3 into	6 together	

Exercise 3

1 F	4 T	7 T
2 T	5 F	8 F
3 F	6 F	

Exercise 4

1 C	3 A	5 E
2 D	4 B	

Exercise 5

1 E	3 F	5 A
2 B	4 C	6 D

Exercise 6

1 E	3 F	5 D
2 C	4 B	6 A

Exercise 7

1 let in	4 put together
2 put back	5 throw away
3 lit up	6 looking for

Exercise 8

- I arrived very late at the hotel last night, and the doors were locked. Thankfully one of the hotel workers <u>let me in</u>!
- I wasn't sure at first how to <u>turn on</u> the shower in the hotel. Then I spent half an hour <u>looking for</u> the switch to <u>turn</u> it <u>off</u>!
- Tokyo looks amazing! At night the city is completely <u>lit up</u> with neon lights.
- It's great that I can just <u>put</u> a coin in the machine and then choose a hot or ice cold coffee!

1 One of the hotel workers let Jessica into the hotel.

2 She couldn´t let herself in because the doors were locked.

3 She had difficulty turning on the shower.

4 It took her half an hour to turn the shower off.

5 Neon lights light up the city at night.

6 She needs to put a coin in the machine to get a coffee.

3 Movement and change

Exercise 1

1	up	3	back	5	back
2	out	4	along	6	up

Exercise 2

1	C	3	F	5	E
2	A	4	D	6	B

Exercise 3

1	T	3	F	5	F
2	T	4	T	6	F

Exercise 4

1 come through   4 coming up
2 came in   5 made for
3 coming off   6 returned to

Exercise 5

1 come back   4 started out
2 went over   5 get (it) back
3 coming along

Exercise 6

1 brought up   4 ended up
2 come off   5 make for
3 started out   6 return to

Exercise 7

1	E	3	B	5	F
2	D	4	A	6	C

Exercise 8

I <u>grew up</u> in a small village. When I was still young, my father didn't <u>come back</u> from the war, so my mother had to <u>bring</u> me <u>up</u> on her own. When I was older, I had to <u>leave</u> my mother <u>behind</u> to look for work in the city. But I knew I could return to the village to visit my family and friends. When I <u>started out</u> living in the city, I had no money. But now I have my own small software company, and the business is really <u>coming along</u>. In fact I've just bought a new house and I can't wait to <u>move in</u>!

1 Reza grew up in a small village.
2 His father didn´t come back from the war.
3 His mother brought Reza up.
4 Reza had to leave his mother behind to look for work in the city.
5 Yes, it is.
6 No, he isn´t.

4 Communication

Exercise 1

1 back to   4 back
2 for   5 for
3 back to   6 back

Exercise 2

1	on	4	out
2	back	5	down
3	back	6	to

Exercise 3

1	C	3	F	5	E
2	A	4	B	6	D

Exercise 4

1	A	3	E	5	F
2	D	4	C	6	B

Exercise 5

1 get back to   4 hang on
2 make out   5 talk to
3 called (Stefan) back   6 call up

Exercise 6

1 telephone someone = <u>called</u> you <u>up</u>
2 say you would like to have something = <u>ask</u> you <u>for</u>
3 manage to hear something = <u>make out</u>
4 telephone someone for a second time = <u>call</u> me <u>back</u>
5 contact someone again after a short time = <u>getting back to</u> me
6 have a conversation with someone = <u>talk to</u>

Exercise 7

1 make out   4 hanging on
2 turn down   5 hold back
3 come back to   6 put (it) to

Exercise 8

I'd like to make a complaint about your customer service. I was told that if there was a problem with my order, I should <u>call up</u> the customer service department and <u>talk to</u> someone about it. Well, when someone eventually answered the phone, I was told to <u>hold on</u> while they found my order details. After half an hour of <u>hanging on</u>, nobody had <u>got back to</u> me, so I ended the conversation. I was hoping to <u>hear from</u> you again but nobody has <u>called</u> me <u>back</u> yet. I might have to put my complaint to them in writing now.

1 The caller wanted to have a conversation with someone in the customer service department.
2 The caller had to hold on.
3 The caller had half an hour before ending the phone call.
4 The caller expected that someone would call back.
5 No, the caller hadn´t had any response from anyone.
6 The caller intends to write a letter of complaint.

5 Giving information

Exercise 1

1	with	4	out	7	out
2	off	5	to	8	in
3	up with	6	up		

Exercise 2

1 A		**3** E		**5** C	
2 D		**4** B		**6** F	

Exercise 3

1 C	**4** A	**7** H	
2 E	**5** f	**8** G	
3 D	**6** B		

Exercise 4

1 writes in	**4** referred to
2 bring up	**5** sums the job up
3 begin with	**6** started off

Exercise 5

1 The findings are <u>based on</u> five years of scientific research.

2 Ahmed had <u>come up with</u> another good idea.

3 All confidential details have been <u>cut out</u> of the report.

4 Dana didn't want to <u>leave out</u> any important details.

5 I would <u>sum up</u> the show as dull and predictable.

6 She <u>refers to</u> him as her partner.

Exercise 6

1 wrote (the answer) in	**4** come up with
2 began with	**5** put forward
3 based on	**6** started off

Exercise 7

1 sums up	**4** put forward
2 dealt with	**5** cut out
3 based on	**6** leave out

Exercise 8

Your report should be <u>based on</u> factual evidence. <u>Begin with</u> a short introduction in which you <u>put forward</u> your main argument. You can <u>leave out</u> smaller details at this point. Then move onto your first topic. Try to <u>come up with</u> at least three topics which <u>deal with</u> different areas. If there are more than five areas, you may wish to <u>cut out</u> some of them or refer to them only briefly. To finish your report, <u>sum up</u> the main points and give a short conclusion.

1 F	**4** T	**7** F
2 F	**5** T	**8** F
3 T	**6** T	

6 Planning and organizing

Exercise 1

1 up	**2** out	**3** on	**4** into

Exercise 2

1 out	**3** up	**5** for
2 about	**4** off	**6** on

Exercise 3

1 B	**3** E	**5** A
2 D	**4** C	

Exercise 4

1 D	**3** A	**5** B
2 C	**4** F	**6** E

Exercise 5

1 finish

2 find out more or do more about it

3 are

4 unsuitable

5 unreliable

6 unexpected

Exercise 6

1 fit me in	**3** wind up	**5** start on
2 aimed at	**4** turn out	**6** go about

Exercise 7

1 followed up	**3** run into	**5** turn out
2 go about	**4** set out	**6** set out

Exercise 8

1 <u>go about</u> = start to deal with something

2 <u>start on</u> = begin to do something

3 <u>line up</u> = arrange to be ready

4 <u>rely on</u> = expect something to happen

5 <u>wind up</u> = end up

6 <u>pull it off</u> = do it successfully

7 Discussions

Exercise 1

1 down	**3** by	**5** out to	**7** to
2 down to	**4** into	**6** out of	**8** back on

Exercise 2

1 I didn't want to go out after work, but my colleagues <u>insisted on</u> it.

2 The guide <u>pointed out</u> all the places of interest along the journey.

3 Okay, I'll join the committee. I didn't want to, but you've managed to <u>talk</u> me <u>into</u> it!

4 She <u>won</u> the interviewers <u>over</u> with her excellent presentation.

5 Nobody agrees with the manager's decision, but he refuses to <u>back down</u>.

6 When it <u>comes round</u> to working overtime, everyone wants to make their opinions heard.

7 She had strong beliefs and always <u>stood by</u> her decisions.

8 I can't <u>go back on</u> my word.

Exercise 3

1 F		**3** D		**5** B	
2 C		**4** A		**6** E	

Exercise 4

1 T		**3** F		**5** T	
2 F		**4** T		**6** T	

Exercise 5

1 B		**4** E		**7** H	
2 C		**5** F		**8** G	
3 D		**6** A			

Exercise 6

1 pointed out

2 listen to

3 go into

4 backed (his argument) up

5 talk (her) out of (it)

6 talked (me) into (doing it)

Exercise 7

Josh: I <u>agree with</u> most the points the author makes, but not all of them.

Ryan: He didn't <u>win</u> me <u>over</u> with his argument at all. He just didn't <u>back up</u> any of his claims with facts or research.

Josh: But if you <u>listen to</u> what he said about how technology has changed society, you have to <u>agree with</u> him.

Ryan: No, for me it all <u>comes down to</u> money – that's what really matters.

1 No, he doesn´t.

2 No, he doesn´t.

3 He thinks the author failed to back up his claims with facts or research.

4 He agrees with the author on how technology has changed society.

5 Money is the most important issue for Ryan.

Exercise 8

1 gave in

2 back up

3 go into

4 insisted on

5 listening to

6 bring (a new topic) into (the debate)

7 stand by

---

8 Advice or warnings

Exercise 1

1 come		**3** pull	
2 keep		**4** stuck	

5 watch

6 messed

7 settle

8 give

Exercise 2

1 out		**3** down		**5** up	
2 with		**4** to		**6** for	

Exercise 3

1 D		**3** F		**5** B	
2 A		**4** C		**6** E	

Exercise 4

1 D		**3** A		**5** B	
2 E		**4** F		**6** C	

Exercise 5

1 OVER		**3** OUT		**5** OVER	
2 OUT		**4** TO		**6** OUT	

Exercise 6

1 come on		**5** stick to
2 watch out		**6** mess up
3 keep to		**7** settle (her) down
4 keep from		**8** given up

Exercise 7

1 pulled (me) over		**4** stick with
2 step up		**5** Come on
3 keep from		

Exercise 8

Dear Ali,

My parents have always encouraged me to <u>try for</u> medical school, but I think I may have <u>messed up</u> the entrance exam. I just don't know who to <u>turn to</u> for help or what to do next. Can you help?

Jack

Dear Jack,

Don't let one failure <u>keep you from</u> doing what you want to do. If going to medical school is your dream, then you should <u>stick with</u> it. <u>Step up</u> your efforts to make sure you get a place in another school. You can do it!

Ali

1 T		**3** T		**5** T	
2 F		**4** F		**6** T	

---

9 Thinking and knowing

Exercise 1

1 back		**3** out	
2 of		**4** about	

Exercise 2

1 out		**4** of		**7** by	
2 about		**5** out		**8** back	
3 of		**6** on			

Exercise 3

1 Have you <u>heard</u> anything more <u>about</u> the bus strike next weekend?

2 It's a tradition that <u>goes back</u> to the 17th century.

3 I can't <u>work out</u> how to switch on this machine.

4 What advice will you <u>pass on</u> to your children one day?

5 As soon as I hear that music, memories <u>come back</u> to me.

6 I'll never forget it. It's something that will always <u>stick in</u> my mind.

7 He <u>looks back</u> on his school days very fondly.

8 I'm <u>thinking of</u> starting my own business.

Exercise 4

1	C	3	E	5	A
2	F	4	D	6	B

Exercise 5

1	T	4	T	7	F
2	F	5	F	8	F
3	T	6	F		

Exercise 6

1 brings back memories of

2 figure out

3 go back

4 think of

5 know much about

6 go by

Exercise 7

1	goes by	5	come back
2	stuck in	6	brought back
3	passed on	7	dates back
4	heard of	8	handed down

Exercise 8

1 has existed since = <u>goes back to</u>

2 makes me think about = <u>reminds</u> me <u>of</u>

3 give or teach = <u>pass on</u>

4 understand more regarding = <u>know</u> more <u>about</u>

5 continues clearly in = <u>sticks in</u>

6 passed = <u>gone by</u>

---

10 Feelings

Exercise 1

1	B	3	A
2	D	4	C

Exercise 2

1	get over	5	calm down
2	hoping for	6	get to you
3	relate to	7	open up
4	looking forward to	8	let down

Exercise 3

1	up to	5	to
2	down	6	over
3	with	7	on
4	up	8	for

Exercise 4

1	E	3	C	5	B
2	F	4	D	6	A

Exercise 5

1	E	3	F	5	B
2	D	4	C	6	A

Exercise 6

1	calmed down	4	plays on
2	deal with	5	gone through
3	got over		

Exercise 7

1	open up	4	gone through
2	care for	5	face up to
3	hope for	6	got over

Exercise 8

1 <u>calmed down</u> = become less upset

2 <u>getting over</u> it = recover from

3 <u>face up to</u> = accept and deal with

4 <u>relate to</u> = understand

5 <u>looking forward to</u> = be happy (that something is going to happen)

6 <u>cheer</u> me <u>up</u> = stop feeling sad and become happier

---

11 Attitudes

Exercise 1

1	B	3	D
2	A	4	C

Exercise 2

1	C	3	E	5	D
2	F	4	A	6	B

Exercise 3

1 They would be upset.

2 It is considered negative.

3 You accept them.

4 It is usually not quite what you want.

5 You support that idea.

6 You are criticising that person.

Exercise 4

1	down	5	for
2	off	6	up
3	in	7	up to
4	to	8	for

Exercise 5

1 look at	**5** settle for
2 objected to	**6** showing off
3 picked on	**7** sees (saving money) as
4 walked out	**8** match up to

Exercise 6

1 put up with	**4** believe in
2 seen (him) as	**5** stands for
3 looks at	**6** going for

Exercise 7

1 Jane did not agree with what the company stood for.

2 We see business as being linked closely linked to education.

3 I'm not opposed to the idea of nuclear power.

4 It isn't always easy to live up to such high standards.

5 We just ignore Kevin when he shows off.

6 I usually go for the cheapest option.

7 Jay was always getting at his little brother.

8 He walked out after a furious argument.

Exercise 8

I look up to my science teacher. He never picks on anyone or puts people down, even though he often has to put up with some badly behaved students. We have our first science exam next month. I'm not trying to show off, but he tells me I am a strong student and that he believes in me.

1 Yes, he does.

2 No, he doesn´t.

3 No, they don´t.

4 Viktor has his first science exam.

5 He is trying not to show off.

6 Yes, he does.

12 Relationships

Exercise 1

1 D	**3** F	**5** C
2 A	**4** B	**6** E

Exercise 2

1 down	**4** with
2 for	**5** up for
3 out	**6** out

Exercise 3

1 D	**3** A	**5** E
2 F	**4** C	**6** B

Exercise 4

1 do with	**4** get on
2 settling down	**5** going out
3 depends on	**6** fall out

Exercise 5

1 D	**4** A	**7** B
2 E	**5** H	**8** C
3 G	**6** F	

Exercise 6

1 depends upon	**4** count on
2 get on	**5** falling apart
3 going out	

Exercise 7

1 Sandra is a person you can always depend on to get things done in time.

2 He left the company after he fell out with his manager about salary.

3 You don't have to tell anyone what happened. It has nothing to do with them.

4 I'm sorry. I really want to make up with you.

5 He's very good looking. She fell for him as soon as she met him.

6 Don't walk away in the middle of an argument! I haven't finished with you yet.

Exercise 8

Andrew and I first got together six years ago when we met on holiday. The fact that he's rich has nothing to do with why I fell for him. We just got along so well together, even though he's a lot older than me. What I love about Andrew is that I can rely on him to take care of me. But I don't depend on his money. I have always had plenty of my own!

1 F	**3** F	**5** T
2 F	**4** T	**6** F

13 Socializing and leisure time

Exercise 1

1 up	**3** in
2 out	**4** over

Exercise 2

1 call on	**4** got together
2 come along	**5** hang out
3 drop in	**6** showed up

Exercise 3

1 T	**3** F	**5** F	**7** T
2 T	**4** T	**6** T	**8** F

Exercise 4

1 stay in	**5** go over
2 come over	**6** taken up
3 dropped in	**7** went over
4 shows up	**8** drop in

Exercise 5

1 D	**3** B	**5** C
2 F	**4** A	**6** E

Exercise 6

1 putting (it) off
2 take up
3 get in
4 come along
5 catch up
6 ate out

Exercise 7

1 It was nice seeing you again. We must get together more often.

2 We're going to a the cinema this evening. Would you like to come along with us?

3 What time shall I come over to your place tonight?

4 What time did you get in last night? Was it very late?

5 I don't feel like eating out tonight. I'll stay at home and cook something for dinner instead.

6 I've decided to take up yoga – they say it's a good form of exercise.

Exercise 8

1 make a short visit = come over
2 going with us to the same place = coming along
3 collect = call for
4 leave the house = go out
5 have a meal at a restaurant = eat out
6 meet = get together

14 Sport and fitness

Exercise 1

1 up
2 down
3 out
4 in

Exercise 2

1 D
2 G
3 F
4 E
5 H
6 B
7 A
8 C

Exercise 3

1 down
2 through
3 into
4 up
5 up
6 out

Exercise 4

1 go
2 up
3 keep
4 behind
5 went
6 into

Exercise 5

1 THROUGH
2 UP
3 DOWN
4 BEHIND
5 IN
6 OFF

Exercise 6

1 cut down
2 sped up
3 wear him out
4 joining in
5 keep up
6 slowed down

Exercise 7

1 getting into = becoming interested in

2 work on = make an effort to improve

3 work up = increase something gradually

4 wear myself out = become too tired

5 wake up = become conscious after sleeping

6 work out = do physical exercises

Exercise 8

1 It seemed impossible for him to catch up with the rest of the team.

2 Clark is confident the team can go through to the first division this year.

3 Michael scored just four minutes after they had kicked off.

4 She held the lead early in the race but now she's falling behind.

5 You need to work on/at keeping fit.

6 Start slowly and build up to longer training sessions.

7 Unfortunately the team went down four goals to one.

8 Start getting into the habit of walking to work.

15 Travel and tourism

Exercise 1

1 in
2 across
3 into
4 round
5 off
6 into
7 out
8 on

Exercise 2

1 F
2 D
3 A
4 G
5 B
6 E
7 H
8 C

Exercise 3

1 T
2 F
3 T
4 F
5 F
6 T

Exercise 4

1 get off
2 got off
3 headed for
4 moved on
5 came across
6 went around

Exercise 5

1 AWAY
2 FOR
3 IN
4 ACROSS
5 AWAY
6 AROUND

Exercise 6

1 He's going to go round Europe with a friend for three months.

2 Welcome home! When did you get back from holiday?

3 It's a lovely, sunny day. Let's head to the beach today.

4 You have to get off the bus at the last stop.

5 You can check in online, to save yourself time at the airport.

6 What time does your train get in at the station?

Exercise 7

1 get away   5 get into
2 check out   6 got in
3 come from   7 check in
4 get off   8 drop (passengers) off

Exercise 8

THE GEORGE HOTEL **

Our plane <u>got into</u> London very late – at about 2 a.m. But the staff were friendly and helpful when we <u>checked in</u>. The hotel is ideally located for <u>going around</u> the main tourist attractions in the city centre. We <u>came across</u> an excellent Indian restaurant next door, which I'd recommend. We're planning on <u>getting away</u> for a short holiday next year. I think we will definitely <u>head for</u> the George Hotel!

1 It arrived very late / at 2 a.m.
2 The staff were friendly and helpful.
3 It is a good location for going around the main tourist attractions in the city.
4 They found an excellent Indian restaurant.
5 They are planning a short holiday.
6 They will stay at the George Hotel.

16 Clothing and fashion

Exercise 1

1 up   2 on   3 out   4 off

Exercise 2

1 out   3 up   5 in
2 off   4 with   6 on

Exercise 3

1 F   3 B   5 A
2 D   4 E   6 C

Exercise 4

1 T   3 F   5 F
2 T   4 T   6 F

Exercise 5

1 D   4 H   7 E
2 G   5 B   8 F
3 A   6 C

Exercise 6

1 C   3 B   5 F
2 D   4 E   6 A

Exercise 7

1 dress up
2 got (it) on
3 put on
4 show off
5 did up
6 took (his hat) off

Exercise 8

Isabella: Hi. I'd like to <u>try on</u> this dress, please. I'm not sure about the size, though …

Store Assistant: No problem. You can <u>put</u> it <u>on</u> in the changing room over there. If the dress doesn't fit we can <u>take</u> it <u>in</u> for you.

Isabella: Thanks. Could you <u>pick out</u> some shoes to match the dress?

Store Assistant: Of course. How about these silver shoes? They <u>go</u> really well <u>with</u> it.

Isabella: Oh yes, they're much nicer than the shoes I <u>have on</u>!

1 T   4 F
2 F   5 T
3 T   6 T

17 Studying and learning

Exercise 1

1 up   3 through   5 to
2 out   4 for   6 behind

Exercise 2

1 B   3 H   5 D   7 F
2 E   4 C   6 A   8 G

Exercise 3

1 up   3 through   5 out
2 out   4 out   6 in

Exercise 4

1 You choose to do it.
2 You give it to someone.
3 You agree to become involved with it.
4 You are below the standard of others.
5 You examine it closely.
6 You do it quickly.

Exercise 5

1 cut out
2 fall behind
3 handed in
4 looks at
5 missed (a few things) out
6 run through

Exercise 6

1 looking through
2 missed (it) out
3 run through
4 mix up
5 looks at
6 take in
7 finding out
8 went over

Exercise 7

1 not reach the same standard or level as other people = <u>fall behind</u>

2 signed an agreement to do a course of study = <u>signed up</u>

3 understand something = <u>take in</u>

4 learn something = <u>find out</u>

5 helped me to understand something by talking about it = <u>went over</u>

6 decided to do something = <u>opted for</u>

Exercise 8

1 signed up	4 find out
2 running over	5 dropped out
3 relate to	6 hand in

18 Jobs and careers

Exercise 1

1 T	3 T	5 T
2 F	4 F	6 T

Exercise 2

1 B	3 E	5 D
2 A	4 F	6 C

Exercise 3

1 stay on	5 shut (it) down
2 stick (it) out	6 made up of
3 moving into	7 step down
4 got (very little) out of	8 walked out

Exercise 4

1 set up	5 make up
2 carry out	6 shut down
3 get out of	7 stick out
4 step down	8 shut down

Exercise 5

1 UP	4 INTO
2 IN	5 OUT OF
3 ON	6 OUT

Exercise 6

1 Do you have everything you need in order to <u>carry out</u> the task?

2 We regret to announce that we have to <u>lay off</u> some members of staff.

3 We're <u>taking on</u> three new employees this month.

4 She's not happy in her work, but she's decided to <u>stick it out</u> until she finds something else.

5 She used to work in the public sector but she's <u>moved into</u> the private sector now.

6 Are you the kind of person who will be able to <u>fit in</u> with our way of doing things?

Exercise 7

1 D	3 C	5 B
2 A	4 E	6 F

Exercise 8

1 <u>fit in</u> = be happy and accepted by people

2 <u>stand out</u> = be noticeable and different to other things

3 <u>take</u> you <u>on</u> = employ you

4 <u>set up</u> = started

5 <u>carrying out</u> = doing

6 <u>take on</u> = accept

19 Business

Exercise 1

1 on	3 off	5 down
2 out	4 up	6 over

Exercise 2

1 up	3 off	5 off
2 up	4 out	6 down

Exercise 3

1 D	4 F	7 E
2 A	5 B	8 G
3 C	6 H	

Exercise 4

1 OVER	4 OVER
2 UP	5 UP
3 OFF	6 AROUND

Exercise 5

1 built on	4 taken over
2 pull out	5 turn (things) around
3 starting up	6 look into

Exercise 6

1 turn around	4 look into it
2 send out	5 take over
3 to pull out of	6 trying out

Exercise 7

I <u>started up</u> my own business three years ago. At first things really <u>took off</u> – I was making lots of money and the customers were happy with my products. I tried hard to <u>build on</u> my good relationship with customers. But the economy is weak now, so people are less willing to <u>hand over</u> money. We'll need to <u>keep</u> our costs <u>down</u> for the business to survive another year. I really hope the economy <u>turns around</u> soon.

1 He started his business three years ago.

2 Yes, it was.

3 He tried to take advantage of his good relationship with customers

4 They don´t want to spend money now because the economy is weak.

5 He must keep costs at a low level.

6 He hopes the economy will improve.

Exercise 8

1 make up for

2 send out

3 trying out

4 come out of

5 hand over

6 teamed up

20 Money and spending

Exercise 1

1 to	**3** off	**5** off
2 into	**4** down	**6** aside

Exercise 2

1 B	**3** E	**5** D
2 F	**4** A	**6** C

Exercise 3

1 taking out	**4** sold off
2 cut back on	**5** added up to
3 pay for	**6** brings in

Exercise 4

1 F	**3** C	**5** E
2 D	**4** B	**6** A

Exercise 5

1 OFF	**3** OUT	**5** IN
2 ON	**4** DOWN	**6** UP

Exercise 6

1 In order to save money, we are <u>cutting back on</u> unnecessary stationery.

2 It took us a while to <u>build up</u> a large database, but we've succeeded in that now.

3 How are you ever going to <u>pay off</u> all these expensive things you've bought on your credit card?

4 Having too many credit cards is a common way for people to <u>get into</u> debt.

5 She's <u>come into</u> some money and has bought a huge house in the south of France.

6 It's a good idea to <u>set aside</u> some money for when you have retired.

Exercise 7

1 paying in	**4** cut back on
2 give away	**5** brings in
3 came into	**6** built up

Exercise 8

If you're looking to <u>put down</u> a deposit on a house, you might think you can't afford it, but there are things you can do to help. <u>Cutting back on</u> luxuries you don't need is a great way to <u>build up</u> your savings. You might also

want to consider <u>taking out</u> a loan to help cover the cost of a large deposit. Remember, if you do <u>get into</u> debt, don't worry – there are companies out there who can help you to <u>pay</u> it <u>off</u>.

1 T	**3** T	**5** F
2 F	**4** T	

21 Reporting in the media

Exercise 1

1 OFF	**4** WITH
2 IN	**5** FROM
3 INTO	**6** UNDER

Exercise 2

1 about	**4** about
2 into	**5** up
3 under	**6** with

Exercise 3

1 T	**3** T	**5** T
2 T	**4** F	**6** F

Exercise 4

1 looking for	**4** brought about
2 runs through	**5** put out
3 step in	**6** make up

Exercise 5

Environmental campaigners have <u>called for</u> a ban on traffic in the city centre. This <u>comes after</u> pollution levels were found to be dangerously high for two years running. The campaigners' plans to <u>turn</u> the city centre <u>into</u> a car-free zone have <u>met with</u> support from city residents. Campaign spokesman Derek Shields said: 'Closing the city centre to traffic would <u>result in</u> lower carbon emissions and make the city a more pleasant place to live. It's time for the city authorities to <u>step in</u> and address this problem.'

1 cause a situation or event to happen = <u>result in</u>

2 get involved in a situation and try to help = <u>step in</u>

3 happens or exists later than a particular event or point in time = <u>comes after</u>

4 change something and make it become another thing = <u>turn ... into</u>

5 got a particular reaction = <u>met with</u>

6 demanded that an action should be done = <u>called for</u>

Exercise 6

1 World leaders have <u>called for</u> action after the news of the attack.

2 Although the company hadn't made a formal announcement, word soon <u>got around</u> that the director had resigned.

3 A ripple of excitement <u>ran through</u> the football fans as their hero came on to the pitch.

4 Eventually the army had to <u>step in</u> and offer assistance to the flood victims.

5 Minutes after the explosion, panic <u>set in</u> and people began to flee the building.

6 The headmaster decided it was time to <u>call in</u> the police to sort out the problem of theft in the school.

Exercise 7

1	D	**3**	F	**5**	B
2	A	**4**	E	**6**	C

Exercise 8

1	calling for	**5**	met with
2	called in	**6**	result from
3	call off	**7**	resulted in
4	got round	**8**	turn into

22 Political events

Exercise 1

1	by	**5**	for
2	back	**6**	into
3	down	**7**	ahead
4	in	**8**	out

Exercise 2

1	with	**4**	into
2	on	**5**	out
3	ahead	**6**	for

Exercise 3

1	C	**4**	A	**7**	G
2	E	**5**	H	**8**	F
3	B	**6**	D		

Exercise 4

1	DOWN	**4**	AHEAD
2	INTO	**5**	BY
3	BACK	**6**	IN

Exercise 5

1	dealing with	**4**	bring in
2	imposed (restrictions) on	**5**	engage in
3	lead to	**6**	pull (troops) out

Exercise 6

1	fight back	**4**	pulled out
2	go ahead	**5**	bring down
3	sort out	**6**	bring in

Exercise 7

1 We're <u>cracking down</u> hard on vigilante groups in general.

2 The new measures are designed to <u>deal with</u> immigration more effectively.

3 The agreement will <u>lead to</u> better relationships between the two countries.

4 The government will not <u>stand by</u> and allow thieves to operate in this way.

5 NATO <u>stands for</u> North Atlantic Treaty Organization.

6 Campaigners are <u>pressing for</u> a review of the current law.

7 The state dominates the groups and <u>imposes</u> its directives <u>on</u> them.

8 The two countries are <u>engaged in</u> a border dispute.

Exercise 8

1 <u>entered into</u> = became involved in something

2 <u>push for</u> = try to persuade other people to help you achieve something

3 <u>impose ... upon</u> = use authority to force someone to accept something

4 <u>engage in</u> = take part in something

5 <u>stand by</u> = allow something to happen

6 <u>standing for</u> = being a candidate in an election

23 Crime

Exercise 1

1	up	**3**	up
2	away	**4**	off

Exercise 2

1	in	**5**	up
2	into	**6**	for
3	up	**7**	away
4	in	**8**	down

Exercise 3

1	T	**4**	T	**7**	T
2	F	**5**	T	**8**	F
3	T	**6**	F		

Exercise 4

1	E	**4**	H	**7**	F
2	G	**5**	B	**8**	D
3	A	**6**	C		

Exercise 5

1	broke into	**4**	handed (it) in
2	got away	**5**	locked (him) in
3	get (him) off	**6**	running away

Exercise 6

1	C	**3**	F	**5**	A
2	E	**4**	B	**6**	D

Exercise 7

1	IN	**3**	FOR	**5**	DOWN
2	OFF	**4**	UP	**6**	AWAY

Exercise 8

A man who <u>held up</u> a bank in the city centre has been arrested by police. The man <u>locked</u> staff <u>in</u> a store room while he attempted to <u>break into</u> the safe. When the safe would not open, he tried to <u>run away</u>. But police arrived in time to stop him. Police chief Dean Sanchez said: 'He was foolish to think he could <u>get away with</u> this.' Three other men have been <u>taken in</u> for questioning.

1 He tried to rob a bank.

2 Staff could not leave the store room because they were locked in.

3 He tried to enter the safe illegally.

4 He tried to leave because the safe would not open.

5 The man was foolish to think that he could get away with this.

6 The police have made three other men go to the police station.

24 Disaster and destruction

Exercise 1

1 DOWN	4 TO
2 UP	5 OUT
3 OFF	6 OUT

Exercise 2

1 H	4 C	7 A
2 G	5 E	8 D
3 F	6 B	

Exercise 3

1 smash down	4 blew up
2 put out	5 going off
3 wipe out	6 run out

Exercise 4

1 D	4 B	7 C
2 E	5 F	8 G
3 F	6 H	

Exercise 5

1 The wind <u>blew away</u> all the papers on my desk.

2 My car <u>broke down</u> on the way to work.

3 After the petrol shortage, petrol supplies have all <u>run out</u>.

4 The earthquake caused large parts of the building to <u>fall down</u>.

5 It took fire fighters several days to <u>put out</u> the fire.

6 She <u>wrote off</u> the car when she crashed into a wall.

Exercise 6

1 blew away	4 reduced to
2 blown up	5 going off
3 broke down	6 run down

Exercise 7

1 A	3 B	5 C
2 B	4 C	6 A

Exercise 8

A forest fire that <u>broke out</u> on a farm three days ago is now under control. Firefighters were <u>running out</u> of water supplies yesterday, but helicopters brought extra supplies to help <u>put out</u> the blaze. Huge areas of forest have been virtually <u>wiped out</u> by the fire. Many farm buildings were also <u>reduced to</u> rubble. Fortunately the fire did not spread to a nearby town, which could have <u>cut</u> the town <u>off</u> from firefighters.

1 T	3 F	5 F
2 T	4 T	6 F

25 Helping and recovering

Exercise 1

1 on	5 with
2 up	6 down
3 out	7 around
4 from	8 in

Exercise 2

1 C	3 A	5 D
2 F	4 B	6 E

Exercise 3

1 F	3 T	5 T
2 F	4 F	6 F

Exercise 4

1 AROUND	3 AFTER	5 FROM
2 BEHIND	4 WITH	6 OUT

Exercise 5

1 clean up

2 protect (yourself) from

3 live with

4 held on to

5 kept on

6 settled down

Exercise 6

1 It was difficult for him to <u>carry on</u> after the accident.

2 I just don't know how we're going to <u>get through</u> this difficult time.

3 If there's anything I can do to <u>help out</u>, just let me know.

4 Things will get better – You just need to keep <u>holding on</u>!

5 Dario really wanted to <u>leave</u> his past <u>behind</u> and move on with life.

6 I offered to <u>look after</u> Helen's children while she's in hospital.

7 After a few hours, his stomach <u>settled down</u> and he ate a sandwich.

8 They <u>took in</u> a homeless couple for a week while they looked for a place to stay.

Exercise 7

1 stopped having a past feeling and progressed to something new = <u>left</u> that part of my life <u>behind</u>

2 took care of me = <u>looked after</u> me

3 survive something = <u>get through</u>

4 did something to help me = <u>helped</u> me <u>out</u>

5 changed my life completely and made it better = <u>turned</u> my life <u>around</u>

6 allowed me to live at her house = <u>took</u> me <u>in</u>

Exercise 8

1 look after

2 settled down

3 hold on to / hold onto

4 keep on / carry on

5 clean up

6 took in

Index

The numbers refer to the unit numbers.

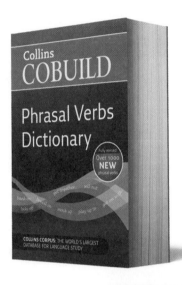